Cultural Expertise

Cultural Expertise

An Emergent Concept and Evolving Practices

Special Issue Editor
Livia Holden

MDPI • Basel • Beijing • Wuhan • Barcelona • Belgrade

Special Issue Editor
Livia Holden
University of Oxford
UK

Editorial Office
MDPI
St. Alban-Anlage 66
4052 Basel, Switzerland

This is a reprint of articles from the Special Issue published online in the open access journal *Laws* (ISSN 2075-471X) in 2019 (available at: https://www.mdpi.com/journal/laws/special_issues/culture_law).

For citation purposes, cite each article independently as indicated on the article page online and as indicated below:

LastName, A.A.; LastName, B.B.; LastName, C.C. Article Title. *Journal Name* **Year**, *Article Number*, Page Range.

ISBN 978-3-03928-050-6 (Pbk)
ISBN 978-3-03928-051-3 (PDF)

Cover image courtesy of Marius Holden.

© 2020 by the authors. Articles in this book are Open Access and distributed under the Creative Commons Attribution (CC BY) license, which allows users to download, copy and build upon published articles, as long as the author and publisher are properly credited, which ensures maximum dissemination and a wider impact of our publications.
The book as a whole is distributed by MDPI under the terms and conditions of the Creative Commons license CC BY-NC-ND.

Contents

About the Special Issue Editor vii

Livia Holden
Cultural Expertise: An Emergent Concept and Evolving Practices
Reprinted from: *Laws* **2019**, *8*, 28, doi:10.3390/laws8040028 1

Anna Ziliotto
Cultural Expertise in Italian Criminal Justice: From Criminal Anthropology to Anthropological Expert Witnessing
Reprinted from: *Laws* **2019**, *8*, 13, doi:10.3390/laws8020013 5

Aurelien Bouayad
The Cactus and the Anthropologist: The Evolution of Cultural Expertise on the Entheogenic Use of Peyote in the United States
Reprinted from: *Laws* **2019**, *8*, 12, doi:10.3390/laws8020012 23

Annika Rabo
Cultural Expertise in Sweden: A History of Its Use
Reprinted from: *Laws* **2019**, *8*, 22, doi:10.3390/laws8030022 45

Ilenia Ruggiu
The "Cultural Test" as Cultural Expertise: Evolution of a Legal–Anthropological Tool for Judges
Reprinted from: *Laws* **2019**, *8*, 15, doi:10.3390/laws8030015 58

Aisha Fofana Ibrahim
The Bondo Society as a Political Tool: Examining Cultural Expertise in Sierra Leone from 1961 to 2018
Reprinted from: *Laws* **2019**, *8*, 17, doi:10.3390/laws8030017 73

About the Special Issue Editor

Livia Holden (Ph.D.—School of Oriental and African Studies University of London) is Senior Research Fellow at the Centre for Socio-Legal Studies, University of Oxford, where she leads the European Research Council's funded project Cultural Expertise in Europe: What Is It Useful For? (EURO-EXPERT) and a project funded by Global Challenges Research Funds, UK Gender Sensitisation for Judicial Education in Pakistan and Indonesia. She is a tenured Full Professor at the University of Padua (on leave) and Research Associate at the Centre of History and Anthropology of Law (CHAD) at Paris Nanterre University. She is an SCR Member and College Advisor at St Antony's College. She regularly provides expert opinions for cases pertaining to immigration law, family law, and criminal law in the United Kingdom, United States, and the Netherlands. Prior to Oxford, she was Dean of the Humanities and Social Sciences Faculty and Professor of Anthropology at the Karakoram International University, Professor of Anthropology at Lahore University of Management Sciences, Lecturer in International Human Rights and Research Fellow at the Socio-Legal Research Centre at Griffith University, Research Fellow at Freie University, and Visiting Professor at Humboldt University Berlin and INALCO Paris. She has been 2015/16 Fellow at the Institute for Advanced Studies in Nantes and 2016 Social Sciences Awardee of the Pakistan Inter-University Consortium for the Promotion of Social Sciences. She holds affiliations with the Center for the Study of Law and Society at the University of California Berkeley and Otago University.

Editorial

Cultural Expertise: An Emergent Concept and Evolving Practices

Livia Holden

CSLS, Faculty of Law, University of Oxford, Oxford OX13UQ, UK; livia.holden@csls.ox.ac.uk

Received: 4 November 2019; Accepted: 5 November 2019; Published: 8 November 2019

Abstract: This introduction provides a snapshot on cultural expertise as an emergent concept in the socio-legal studies and evolving practices in the formulation of rights and the resolution of conflicts in and out of court. It starts with the definition of cultural expertise and the need for an integrated and broad conceptualization that includes all the arrays of socio-legal instruments that use knowledge from the social sciences to assist decision-making authorities in the settlement of conflicts. It then mentions the wide span of fields of cultural expertise going from the recognition of the rights of autochthone minorities and the First Nations to the politics of cultural expertise in modern reformulations of customs, vis-à-vis gender rights, including the revisitation of socio-legal instruments such as the cultural test and the scrutiny of psychiatric evaluation in criminal trials. It concludes by offering short descriptions of the papers included in the Special Issue, which include judicial practices involving cultural experts and surveys of the most frequent fields of expert witnessing that are related to the culture. In addition, it interrogates who the experts are; how cultural expert witnessing has been received; how cultural expertise has developed across the sister disciplines; and finally, it asks whether academic truth and legal truth are commensurable.

Keywords: socio-legal studies; anthropology of law; law and society; multicultural societies; cross-cultural dispute resolution; cultural expertise; cultural defense; cultural test; Sweden; Italy; Sami; First Nations

---

Cultural expertise in the form of expert opinions formulated by social scientists appointed as experts in court and out of court for dispute resolution and the claim of rights is not different from any other kind of expertise used for the facilitation of dispute resolution. In specialized fields of law, such as native land titles and First Nations' rights in America and Australia, the appointment of social scientists as experts, especially anthropologists, dates back to the 19th century. Social scientists have played an active role in policymaking in the United Kingdom and America for more than 200 years. In the contemporary management of migration fluxes, the appointment of anthropologists as country experts has become increasingly frequent in common law and civil law countries for immigration proceedings. On the one hand, doubts and concerns exist regarding the usefulness and appropriateness of social sciences, and in particular anthropology, for dispute resolution; while on the other, existing conceptual tools do not allow an encompassing analysis of the use of socio–anthropological knowledge in the legal field, especially for what concerns the usefulness of social scientists as expert witnesses. A first definition of cultural expertise described it as "the special knowledge that enables socio-legal scholars, or, more generally speaking, cultural mediators—the so-called cultural brokers—to locate and describe relevant facts in light of the particular background of the claimants and litigants and for the use of the court" (Holden 2011). However, this definition is too restrictive today because it does not account for the broader range of out-of-court procedures in which the knowledge of the social sciences is applied to the resolution of conflicts, litigation, and the formulation of rights—hence, the need for an integrated definition of cultural expertise that takes into account both in-court and out-of-court conflicts and connects with the current debates on the impact of social sciences in society (Holden 2019).

Hence, I propose a newly formulated definition of cultural expertise as special knowledge that enables socio-legal scholars, experts in laws and cultures, and cultural mediators—the so-called cultural brokers—to locate and describe relevant facts, in light of the particular background of the claimants/litigants/accused and for the use of conflict resolution or the decision-making authority (See also Holden 2020). Although this definition of cultural expertise is new, the practices that this concept describes are not and the socio-legal literature has already developed articulated reflections on specific aspects, concepts, and practices that refer to the use of cultural knowledge in law.[1] This Special Issue focuses on the contemporary evolution and variation of cultural expertise as an emergent concept providing a conceptual umbrella to a variety of evolving practices, all of which include the use of the special knowledge of social sciences for the resolution of conflicts. It surveys the application of cultural expertise in the legal process with an unprecedented span of fields going from the recognition of the rights of autochthone minorities and the First Nations to the politics of cultural expertise in modern reformulations of customs, vis-à-vis gender rights, and also includes the revisitation of socio-legal instruments, such as the cultural test and the scrutiny of psychiatric evaluation in criminal trials. This Special Issue stresses in particular the development and change of culture-related expert witnessing over recent times, culture-related adjudication, and the resolution of disputes, criminal litigation, and other kinds of court and out-of-court procedures.

This Special Issue offers descriptions of judicial practices involving cultural experts and surveys of the most frequent fields of expert witness that are related with culture. In addition, it interrogates who the experts are and outlines their links with local communities and that with the courts and the state power and politics; how cultural expert witnessing has been received by judges; how cultural expertise has developed across the sister disciplines of history and psychiatry. Finally, it asks whether academic truth and legal truth are commensurable across time and space, in order to argue for a closer intersectoral collaboration among socio-legal experts and the legal profession and a greater transparency in the practice of cultural expertise.

It opens with "The Cactus and the Anthropologist: The Evolution of Cultural Expertise on the Entheogenic Use of Peyote in the United States" by Aurelien Bouayad. This paper explains the role of anthropologists acting as cultural experts during trials concerning the First Nations and the use of peyote. Bouayad explores historical sources to highlight that anthropologists were not only experts but also political actors, in that some of them took a stance to counterbalance the demonization and prohibition of the medicinal and sacramental use of peyote by First Nations. This paper shows that anthropologists who were experts on the use of peyote among First Nations were deployed as mediators assisting lawmakers and lawyers for their understanding of cultural and religious practices, as well as a advisors of the First Nations for the formulation of rights in legal terms. Bouayad argues that his in-depth study of the peyote controversy highlights the complexity and the articulation of the role of anthropologists as experts, which goes well beyond the role of expert witness in court. He also highlights how the notion of neutrality in court is potentially dangerous and describes the historical instances in which neutrality has, in fact, concealed a bias that enforced and perpetuated discrimination against First Nations. Bouayad concludes by suggesting that the scope of the conceptualization of cultural expertise should be much wider than the court setting in order to also include the role of anthropologists out of court and in the political setting.

"Cultural Expertise in Italian Criminal Justice: From Criminal Anthropology to Anthropological Expert Witnessing" by Anna Ziliotto highlights the differences between the concept of cultural expertise and the psychiatric evaluation in criminal trials developed by Cesare Lombroso at the end of the 19th century. The psychiatric evaluation of the School of Criminal Anthropology looked at criminal behavior as the result of organic causes that undermined any kind of individual autonomy in the appraisal of

---

[1] (As a non-exhaustive list see: van Broeck 2001; Good 2007; Grillo 2016; Lawrance and Ruffer 2015; Renteln 2004; Rosen 1977, 2017; Strijbosch 1991).

legal responsibility. Ziliotto sees the pitfall of Lombroso's theory in its close embedment in the Positive School of Penal Law which inspired the Rocco Penal Code, on which Italy's current penal code is largely based. Ziliotto reminds us that the overvaluation of the psychiatric assessment along with the concomitant disregard of cultural knowledge and individual autonomy was consolidated by the racial ideology of the country's fascist dictatorship. She argues, therefore, for the need of new instruments that are conceptually and methodologically adequate to take into account today's social diversity and highlights the link between law and culture within a framework of intersectoral collaboration between lawyers and anthropologists.

"Cultural Expertise in Sweden: A History of Its Use" by Annika Rabo presents a survey of the practices and a compact case study of cultural expertise in Sweden. Rabo's article shows that the concept of cultural expertise adapts well even in a country that tends to perceive itself as homogeneous yet displays an important variety of pragmatical instruments to integrate the knowledge of the social sciences into the resolution of disputes and the formulation of rights. Rabo has conducted qualitative interviews with cultural experts and lists expert witnesses in court, academicians, interpreters, and mediators. She also includes her own reflections on her experience of acting as an expert witness in court. Rabo shows that there is little awareness in Sweden of all the instruments that fall into the notion of cultural expertise and links this with the limited acknowledgement of Swedish society toward diversity. Yet her data also show an important potential for the application of the concept of cultural expertise within the framework of the experience of experts, lawyers, prosecutors, and courts. The article includes cases concerning the Sami, the Roma, and also recent migration flows from Africa and Asia. Swedish case law ranges from land rights to ethnic discrimination but also includes criminal and asylum cases. Rabo concludes that the widespread ideal of homogeneity and sameness in Sweden leads to the undermining of cultural differences or to interpret differences in a negative way, eventually leading to discrimination. She argues for the need for a cultural expertise that feeds into the judicial practice in the form of interdisciplinary collaboration.

"The "Cultural Test" as Cultural Expertise: Evolution of a Legal–Anthropological Tool for Judges" by Ilenia Ruggiu analyses the cultural test as a creative legal transplant in Italy. The author was inspired by the North American cultural test for legal matters that involve an appraisal of culture and designed a variation thereof to be applied in the context of diversity, following recent migration flows to Italy. The cultural test formulated by Ruggiu is a sequence of questions that judges would ask themselves in order to establish whether culture is relevant to a certain matter and whether so-defined cultural behavior would deserve legal protection. This article also delves into the debates generated in Italy concerning the proposal of the adoption of the cultural test. Ruggiu concludes by reformulating the cultural test as a form of standardized cultural expertise that does not necessitate the appointment of cultural experts because it provides judges with the capacity to become experts themselves.

"The Bondo Society as a Political Tool: Examining Cultural Expertise in Sierra Leone from 1961 to 2018" by Aisha Fofana Ibrahim closes this Special Issue by providing insights into the political backgrounds of cultural expertise in the highly debated topic of FGM/C (Female Genital Mutilation/Circumcision) in Sierra Leone. Ibrahim outlines how women secret societies in Sierra Leone have been concomitantly used by advocates of women's rights and elite male politicians who have instrumentalized women's rights for a personal political agenda. She argues that although this instrumentalization is evident now with the controversy raised over FGM/C, it dates back to pre-independence and is deeply embedded in the Bondo society. Hence, expertise cannot be easily separated from political agendas because each social group competes for political control by supporting their own experts. Ibrahim concludes her paper by arguing that the role of cultural expertise in FGM/C is irretrievably embedded within politics and it is impossible to separate the two in the Bondo society. Hence, when using cultural expertise concerning the topic of FGM/C in Europe, she argues, it is necessary to also delve into the complexity of political alignments in the countries where these practices originate, such as Sierra Leone.

Funding: This special issue is an output of the project titled "Cultural Expertise in Europe: What is it useful for?" (EURO-EXPERT) funded by the European Research Council (ERC) under H2020 (ERC grant agreement no. 681814), Principal Investigator: Livia Holden.

Conflicts of Interest: The author declares no conflict of interest.

References

Good, Anthony. 2007. *Anthropology and Expertise in the Asylum Courts*. Abingdon: Routledge Cavendish.
Grillo, Ralph. 2016. Anthropologists Engaged with the Law (and Lawyers). *Antropologia Pubblica* 2: 3–24.
Holden, Livia, ed. 2011. *Cultural Expertise and Litigation*. Abingdon: Routledge, p. 2.
Holden, Livia, ed. 2019. *Cultural Expertise and Socio-Legal Studies*. Special Issue in Studies of Law, Politics, and Society. Bingley: Emeraldinsight.
Holden, Livia. 2020. Cultural Expertise and Law: An Historical Overview. *Law and History Review* 38: 1–18. [CrossRef]
Lawrance, Benjamin N., and Galya Ruffer. 2015. *Adjudicating Refugee and Asylum Status: The Role of Witness, Expertise, and Testimony*. New York: Cambridge University Press.
Renteln, Alison Dundes. 2004. *The Cultural Defense*. Oxford and New York: Oxford University Press.
Rosen, Lawrence. 1977. The Anthropologist as Expert Witness. *American Anthropologist* 79: 555–78. [CrossRef]
Rosen, Lawrence. 2017. *The Judgement of Culture: Cultural Assumptions in American Law*, 1st ed. London: Routledge.
Strijbosch, Fons. 1991. Culturele delicten in de Molukse gemeenschap. *Nederlands Juristenblad* 16: 666–72.
van Broeck, Jeroen. 2001. Cultural Defence and Culturally Motivated Crimes (Cultural Offences). *European Journal of Crime, Criminal Law and Criminal Justice* 9: 1–32. [CrossRef]

© 2019 by the author. Licensee MDPI, Basel, Switzerland. This article is an open access article distributed under the terms and conditions of the Creative Commons Attribution (CC BY) license (http://creativecommons.org/licenses/by/4.0/).

Article

Cultural Expertise in Italian Criminal Justice: From Criminal Anthropology to Anthropological Expert Witnessing

Anna Ziliotto

Anthropological Sciences, University of Turin, 10124 Turin, Italy; annaziliotto@libero.it

Received: 15 April 2019; Accepted: 17 June 2019; Published: 19 June 2019

Abstract: This article traces the rise and fall of psychiatric evaluation in criminal trials from the School of Criminal Anthropology of the late nineteenth century to the current Italian justice system. Influenced by positivism and by specific theories on human evolution, Cesare Lombroso considered criminal action as the result of organic causes excluding any kind of legal autonomy and responsibility of the accused. The Positive School of Penal Law he founded with Enrico Ferri and Raffaele Garofalo profoundly inspired the Rocco Code, on which the current Italian Penal Code is still based, albeit with revisions and repeals. Drafted in 1930 during the fascist government (1922–1943), the latter has also suffered from racial ideology. In order to assess potential mental illnesses that would exclude the responsibility of the accused, to determine their level of dangerousness and to establish the corresponding security measures introduced by the Rocco Code, Italian criminal justice consolidated the link between penal law and psychiatric instruments. Such faith in psychiatric evaluation, however, has been particularly questioned by the increasing frequency of judicial processes involving members of different cultural communities in Italy since the 1970s. Thus, the predominantly pathological aspects evaluated by forensic psychiatrists have often proved to be conceptually and methodologically inadequate to take fully into account the differences between cultures, as well as the different social and cultural conditions affecting the defendant's behaviour. This paper argues that cultural anthropology is particularly suited as an instrument capable of disclosing the cultural implications of the legal process and encourages the use of cultural expertise as an important tool for the inclusiveness and understanding of diversity.

Keywords: criminal anthropology; psychiatric evaluation; cultural expertise; Italian criminal justice system; legal anthropology

---

1. Introduction

The role that cultural expertise should play in Italian legal proceedings is influenced by the way 'culture' and 'cultural factors' have been interpreted throughout the history of Italian law and codes. The most important turning point dates back to the late nineteenth century, when Italy had just been unified, criminal anthropology was at the pinnacle of its success, and its founder, Cesare Lombroso, set up the Positive School of Penal Law, together with Enrico Ferri and Raffaele Garofalo (Lombroso et al. 1886).

The Positive School contributed significantly to what we would now call 'cultural competences' by proposing a pioneering idea: it strongly promoted the engagement of social sciences in the Italian penal law system. The Positive School was persuaded that the competences and the analytical tools of social sciences were capable of comprehending both the crime as a social phenomenon and the complexity of criminal behaviour as a result of both an individual and a social dimension.

Criminal anthropology and the Positive School deeply inspired and shaped the so-called Rocco Code, drawn up by the then Minister of Justice Alfredo Rocco in 1930 and on which the current Italian

Penal Code is based, albeit with adjustments, revisions, and repeals. The Rocco Code, in fact, was the second Penal Code to be drafted after the unification of Italy in 1861, the first one being the so-called Zanardelli Code in 1889, entirely inspired by the liberal principles of the Classic School of Penal Law (Carrara 1867; Ferri 1883). Furthermore, being drafted during the government of Benito Mussolini, the Rocco Code was a partial expression of the fascist ideology, based on the belief that Italy was a nation-state and had one, and only one, racial identity, language and religion. The aim of fascist politics was to strengthen the unity of the nation, which was heavily threatened by the historical, economical, and social inequalities of the South compared to the North.

Consequently, the current Italian criminal justice system is still suffering from the effects of both fascism and the historical and cultural changes of the late nineteenth century, powered by scientific positivism, social and Darwinian evolutionism, and—last but not least—Lombroso's theories about criminals.

Lombroso observed, analysed and classified a great number of criminal and insane people. By interpreting their behaviours as a return to the early stages of human development, he applied the theory of atavism to the study of criminals (Bulferetti 1975; Ferracuti 1996; Frigessi 2003; Gibson and Rafter 2006; Knepper and Ystehede 2013; Lombroso 1921; Montaldo and Tappero 2009; Villa 1985). In his most famous book, *L'uomo delinquente* [*The Criminal Man*], he wrote that the criminal was a man, or a woman, and born criminal, i.e., affected by some kind of mental illness whose signs and manifestations were identifiable inside as well as outside the body. He believed crime was thus a symptom of moral madness (Lombroso 1876; Lombroso and Ferrero 1893). Considered the highest expression of Lombroso's theories as closely related to his scientific approach, criminal anthropology was able to gain an official role inside the Italian penal system at that time.

Precisely because it was based on an interdisciplinary dialogue between law, criminal anthropology and other social sciences, the Positive School managed to revolutionize the Italian criminal justice system by allowing penal law out of the box of exclusively legal studies, positioning it inside sociological ones, and placing the criminal at the heart of penal proceedings. Moreover, contrary to what the Classic School implied—i.e., conceiving crime as corresponding to a violation of moral values—, the Positive School impressed the importance of social defence by giving priority to the 'danger to society' rather than to the moral seriousness of the crime committed by the accused.

Lombroso and the Positive School argued that the responsibility of the accused, and their dangerousness, should be 'measured' by means of an anthropological evaluation based on a bio-psycho analysis. By using data from biology, psychology, psychiatry, statistics and sociology, Lombroso's anthropology—and the role he thought the anthropologist should play as an expert in criminal behaviour—focused on the link between the criminal and their anti-social behaviour as the result of an organic compound and social background together. Consequently, the tools of the psychiatry of the time were used to examine the mental illnesses that might have caused the criminal activity, or to exclude those that may have. Indeed, by meeting the scientific criteria of observation, verifiability and predictability, the psychiatric evaluation was viewed as an objective assessment tool in criminal proceedings. Such a view still persists today.

Having worked on the most proper approach for determining the defendant's level of awareness and dangerousness, and the corresponding security measures to be implemented, the Positive School and the Rocco Code have thus given great importance to the close link between penal law and psychiatry, and to the role of the psychiatrist in criminal trials (Miletti 2007). In their opinion, the Court had to resort to non-arbitrary, objective, and technical requirements, and the right way to assess criminal 'behaviour' technically was offered precisely by forensic psychiatry.

Nevertheless, the supposed objectiveness on which psychiatric evaluation is based has been disturbed by the impact of diasporic communities on the Italian legal system in recent years. Current Italian jurisprudence and social sciences question not only how best to handle cultural differences, but also what forensic psychiatric evaluation lacks in order to be useful when different cultural conditions and origins are to be treated. Since the Italian Code of Criminal Procedure forbids any kind of expertise on the 'personality' of the defendant, except for those assessing their mental disorders which could diminish or completely remove their capacity, the only option to analyse the cultural and behavioural profile of the accused remains psychiatric evaluation.

What so far has prevented cultural anthropologists from taking up an official role as expert consultants in Italian legal proceedings concerns the difficulty in defining and studying 'culture', the lack of regard for culture-related factors inside Italian law and codes, the obstacles that anthropological data encounter in order to be qualified as 'evidence' in the trials as well as the lack of credibility endured by anthropology as a scientific discipline in Italy combined with the criticism of it for having contributed to theories that justified racial distinctions in the past.

The present article aims to reflect at least on three issues. The first concerns the importance of engaging social sciences within the Italian criminal court. The Positive School of Criminal Law and Lombroso's criminal anthropology had already stressed the usefulness of the perspective of social sciences in the late nineteenth century, precisely because they pursued the aim of understanding the complexity of criminal behaviour in its interaction with biological and social factors. The Rocco Code accepted the support of 'auxiliary sciences' only partially while promoting, instead, the contribution of psychiatry and of the other 'hard sciences'. The second point addresses the (claimed) 'objectiveness' on which the forensic psychiatric evaluation is based. In the last few years, defendants belonging to different cultural communities have heavily challenged the faith put in the positive scientific method and on the presumed universality of the 'Western' tools which forensic psychiatry conventionally use to evaluate criminal behaviour. Finally, this article aims to highlight the need for cultural expertise (and particularly anthropological competences) for a better understanding of cultural diversity and in order to improve the current tools being used to evaluate different cultural conducts on trial.

2. The Alliance between Criminal Anthropology and the Positive School

In order to reflect on the engagement of anthropologists as experts of culture-related behaviours in current Italian criminal trials with specific regard to the shortcomings of forensic psychiatric evaluation, what penal law inherited from criminal anthropology and the Positive School needs first to be clearly understood. Therefore, this article is primarily the result of an analytical and historical study of the literature published by Lombroso and by the major exponents of the Positive School of Criminal Law and, secondarily, of the critical analysis and interpretation of the most appropriate bibliography concerning criminal anthropology in Italy.

Anthropology as the study of 'culture' was not a recognized discipline in the middle of the nineteenth century. The first important definition of 'culture' formulated by Edward B. Tylor (Tylor 1871), indeed, dates back to 1871 and cultural anthropology, as a defined discipline, established itself much later in Italy. The anthropology at the time of Lombroso was conceived as 'the natural history of the human being' (Mantegazza 1871, p. 17) and it mainly adopted a biological and physical approach. Paolo Mantegazza, one of the most important (and one of the first to be recognized as such) Italian anthropologists of the middle nineteenth century, said that anthropology 'has no other claims than that of studying the human being with the same experimental criterion with which plants, animals and stones are studied; that it has no other aspiration than that of measuring, weighing the human being and his strengths without the yoke of religious traditions, of preconceived philosophical theories' [non ha altre pretese che quella di studiar l'uomo collo stesso criterio sperimentale con cui si studiano le piante, gli animali, le pietre; che non ha altra aspirazione che quella di misurare, di pesare l'uomo e le sue forze senza il giogo di tradizioni religiose, di teorie filosofiche preconcette] (Mantegazza 1871, pp. 17–18). Contextually, folklore and ethnology (meaning the study of 'exotic' populations around the world, far from 'Western' civilization) developed their researches and techniques of analysis much more slowly (Bernardi 1978; Clemente and Mugnaini 2001; Clemente et al. 1985; Grottanelli 1977; Lombardi Satriani 1980; Puccini 1991). Although these different fields of 'anthropological' studies prolifically dialogued at the turn of the nineteenth century, with the coming of fascism and the so-called 'debate on human races', the biological and cultural approaches gave birth to two different schools of thought.

Therefore, unlike the anthropology based on the studies of human socio-cultural practices, customs and behaviours which developed on one side and is taught in Italian universities today, the anthropology to which Lombroso referred was a science 'studying the human being by means and with the methods of physical sciences, that replaces the dreams of theologians, the fantasies of metaphysicians, with few hard yet real facts ... yet real facts' [che studia l'uomo col mezzo e coi metodi delle scienze fisiche, che ai sogni dei teologi, alle fantasticherie dei metafisici, sostituisce pochi aridi fatti ... ma fatti] (Lombroso 1871, p. 9). This means that Lombroso applied the study of the organic and psychic components of the various human races anthropologists usually undertook in general to the study of the criminal man and woman (Ferri 1892, p. 54).

Even if *L'uomo delinquente* summarizes the key conclusions of criminal anthropology and the modern view of the Italian penal law better than his other works, Lombroso enlightened many fields of study and theories concerning criminals (Lombroso [1864] 1872; Lombroso 1886, 1888, 1909), which widely and quickly spread within, and outside of, Italy for at least three reasons.

Firstly, Lombroso was a great graphomaniac: he wrote many volumes, articles, and essays on what he was studying, discovering and thinking. In addition, he publicized them not only in print, but also by discussing them during his lessons at the Universities of Pavia and Turin as well as in national and international meetings. Lombroso's reputation peaked at the second half of the nineteenth century (Baima Bollone 2003; Colombo 2000; Velo Dalbrenta 2004).

Secondly, Lombroso developed his theories at a time of fervent cultural turmoil. While he was studying 'his' criminal and mad men, Auguste Comte's positivism, and Charles Darwin and Herbert Spencer's theories of evolution were coming to Italy and they would soon revolutionize the Italian scientific, philosophical, and cultural scene (Comte 1831; Darwin 1859; Spencer 1879). According to positivism, human history should have evolved through three stages: the theological one (where people would attribute the causes of natural phenomena to deities), the metaphysical one (where people would attribute the causes of natural phenomena to reason, i.e., to an abstract concept), and finally the scientific one (where reason would identify rules by using observation). In line with this way of thinking, every natural phenomenon would have evolved by means of a close cause-effect relation, and science would have to identify them by using empirical research, experience, and observation.

In addition, theories on social evolution were disseminating quickly. They were based, in brief, on the assumptions of the original unity of human beings, their development by stages, their variability related to their adaptability to the environment, and the inheritance of the characteristics they had acquired (Chiarelli and Pasini 2010; De Lauri 2010; Giacobini and Panattoni 1983; Pancaldi 1983). In line with those theories, Lombroso believed that 'civilization'—meaning the rate of progress achieved by every human population—was one of the causes of insanity. In one of his early books, *Influenza della civiltà su la pazzia e della pazzia su la civiltà* [*The Influence of Civilization on Madness and of Madness on Civilization*], Lombroso (1856, p. 28) argued that 'where civilization has a real impact is on the shape insanity takes. Insanity always shapes itself on the image of civilization in which it rages' [dove veramente influisce la civiltà è nella forma della pazzia. La pazzia si modella sempre su l'imagine della civiltà, in mezzo alla quale imperversa]. So, even if he considered 'civilization' as a synonym of 'culture' (in line with most intellectuals of the time), and he never referred to culture in the same way that we define it nowadays, Lombroso was fascinated from the beginning of his career by the different 'cultural' expressions 'typifying' different human populations. In his works, he repeatedly claimed that criminals were an example of human regression, being like primitive men still living among civilized ones (Lubbock 1865, 1898).

Thirdly, Lombroso's studies on criminals were perceived as important answers to the change Italy was going through as a consequence of its unification in 1861. Their impact on penal law profoundly affected the Italian criminal justice system. In fact, by defining the competences of what he called 'criminal sociology' (Ferri 1892), he established a close link between criminal anthropology and penal law. As he argued,

> [...] by determining the organic and psychic nature of the criminal man and the diverse contributions given by age, gender, marital status, profession, etc. ... to the varied types of crimes, as well as the scientific study of the classes considered dangerous for society, the study of the anthropological factors of crime will provide the judicial police and the very administration of justice itself with the support of new and more secure means for pursuing culprits [lo studio dei fattori antropologici del reato, determinando i caratteri organici e psichici del delinquente ed il vario concorso dell'età, sesso, stato civile, professione ecc ... nelle varie specie di reati, nonché lo studio scientifico sulle classi pericolose della società, offriranno alla polizia giudiziaria ed alla stessa amministrazione della giustizia il sussidio di nuovi e più sicuri mezzi per la ricerca dei colpevoli] (Ferri 1892, p. 624)

By providing the tools to better understand the criminal's bio-psychic behaviour, criminal anthropology, as it was understood, was expected to facilitate the work of the Court.

Being a natural scientist, social physician, forensic psychiatrist, and criminal anthropologist, Lombroso spent his whole life studying the biological factors of mental illness and connecting them to criminal behaviour. By means of criminal anthropology, he intended to find out the organic nature of criminal behaviour by using bio-anthropological data and to give such data a scientific value.

Lombroso's research into the causes of cretinism and pellagra—two very common pathologies in northern Italy in those years, both originated by nutritional deficiencies (cretinism by a lack of iodine and pellagra by a lack of b-group vitamins) and causing dementia and mental illness, which he studied at the beginning of his career—opened his eyes to human behavioural abnormalities and led him to investigate their origin (Lombroso 1870). He had thus started gathering a large amount of data on thieves, bandits, and murderers of the time when he worked as an army medical doctor in Calabria (Lombroso 1898; Milicia 2014). Having many problems related to health and hygiene, illiteracy and poverty due to historical, social and economic reasons, the South of Italy was poorer than the North, and therefore it appeared to Lombroso as a great 'human laboratory' where he could better study criminals.

After his discharge from the army in 1863, he started to give some courses on the clinical and anthropological study of mental diseases at the University of Pavia and at the University of Turin (from 1876) and to work as a medical doctor in the psychiatric hospitals of those cities. There he had the opportunity to observe criminally and mentally insane individuals and to develop his theories on atavism, moral madness and epilepsy with regard to criminal behaviours.

In his studies, he used a positive-scientific method consisting of the empirical observation of human beings, the measurement of their physical and biological attributes, and the comparison and classification of the latter into criminal typologies. His aim was to collect data able not only to describe case-related behaviours, but also to predict and prevent crime. Indeed, by means of observation and thanks to 'the direct, somatic and psychic study of the criminal man comparing him with the findings obtained from the healthy man and the alienated man' [allo studio diretto, somatico e psichico, dell'uomo criminale, confrontandolo colle risultanze offerte dall'uomo sano e dall'alienato] (Lombroso 1876, p. 2), criminal anthropology was deemed capable of producing scientific data.

Consequently, Lombroso claimed his observations and measurements to be at the same time a method and evidence of mental and behavioural anomalies, in order to distinguish between criminals and 'normal' people. In his opinion, every type of mental illness caused specific types of crimes, and such recognition had to be the primary aim of 'his' anthropology.

Just like many other evolutionary biologists and anthropologists in the late nineteenth century, such as Paolo Mantegazza and Giuseppe Sergi, Lombroso believed the study of human morphology (i.e., the measurements of human crania and bodily features in order to benchmark different races, languages, levels of intelligence and capacity for pain and memory, etc.) was the starting point for defining the degree of progress achieved by human beings. They also had in common an interest in phrenology, a discipline based on the supposed link between human morphology and psychology derived from Aristotle's *Physiognomica* (IV century BC) and designed by Franz Joseph Grall in the early nineteenth century (Lombroso 1897; Mantegazza 1876; Puccini 1991; Sergi 1911). More specifically, Lombroso believed that criminals had physical, psychological, and emotional traits close to those of the 'primitive' people studied by his contemporary evolutionary anthropologists far from Europe, and so he placed both criminals and primitive people on the last step of progress and civilization.

Lombroso's perspective was strongly affected by the organicistic approach of nineteenth-century psychiatry. By wanting to overcome the Cartesian (in reality dating back to Plato) dualism of mind and body, the anthropological science studying psychiatric phenomena had to examine the close relationship between the human body and mind, and for that reason it was based precisely on both a biological and psychic analysis.

By examining criminals' bodies and brains, criminal anthropology was specifically intended as a human science that, when facing criminals, had to be able to recognize the signs of their crime. Criminal anthropologists should be able to discover the existence, or otherwise, of injuries which might have altered their ability to discern and thus to live according to social rules. According to Lombroso and the Positive School, the classification of men and women into different criminal typologies had just to simplify the work of the Court. Judges, indeed, would use those criminal categories to recognize criminals, to obtain proof of their nature and to adapt the penalty to their anti-social behaviour.

In order to determine the degree of criminals' responsibilities, the bio-psychic analysis in criminal proceedings had precisely the duty of revealing if the crime was the result of an intentional act or of any kind of mental injury.

In regard to this matter, that is to say with reference to the criminal's free will, the two most important Italian schools of penal law of the late nineteenth century collided.

Inspired by the liberal principles formulated by Cesare Beccaria in his most famous volume, *Dei delitti e delle pene* [*On Crime and Punishments*] published in 1764 (Beccaria [1764] 2001), the Classic School of Penal Law believed that the criminal had the ability of determining themselves and of choosing independently. Fully aware, they had to assume the responsibility for their criminal acts and for having violated social norms. While respecting human dignity, the punishment had to be proportionate to the moral seriousness of the crime committed. Having, indeed, a retributive nature—i.e., its function was to meet the needs of society and to protect its values—, the punishment for the crime committed had to correspond to the capacity of the criminal to understand the social and moral values they had infringed with their actions (Carmignani 1854; Carrara 1867; Lucchini 1886; Marotta 2004; Pessina 1868; Povolo 2007).

Free will is an 'illusion', Ferri said, 'a criminal is not he who wants to be such. In order to commit crimes one needs to have a special physical and moral temperament that either forces one to break the law, or cannot resist outside temptations' [non è delinquente chi vuole. Per commettere delitti bisogna avere una speciale tempra fisica e morale, che o vi spinga, essa, a delinquere o non sappia resistere alle tentazioni esterne] (Lombroso et al. 1886, p. 120).

Indeed, based on Lombroso's criminal anthropology studies and adopting a positive method, the Positive School of Penal Law shifted the focus from the Classic School's idea of crime as a result of violating moral or religious law, to the criminal as a person to be concretely examined. By means of criminal anthropology, criminal sociology and criminal statistics, the Positive School tried to oppose the Enlightenment's idea of crime as the consequence of a sin, committed violating religious laws, or a moral choice, made violating social norms (Ferri 1878, 1881; Garofalo 1880). Depending on biological and pathological causes, the criminal could not have any kind of free will. Given that they were a mad and abnormal individual, indeed, the punishment had to be commensurate with the danger their behaviour might have caused to society rather than with its moral value.

Lombroso actually believed crime to have many causes, such as hereditariness (predominantly), the impact of climate and environment, the influence of 'ethnicity' and civilization, and the consequences deriving from nutrition, age, gender, marital status, profession, education, but it was Ferri (1883, 1892) who clearly theorized the factors conditioning crime. He distinguished between: (1) anthropological or individual factors (i.e., the criminal's organic and psychic constitution and personal characters); (2) physical factors (belonging to the physical environment such as climate, land, weather, etc.); and (3) social factors (i.e., the social environment wherein the criminal lived). Although social factors were involved in all crimes, the Positive School believed the only possible aspect to be proven was the influence of mental illnesses. Thus, the only choice was to reduce and to prevent social factors determining criminality, and that was the main purpose of the Positive School. In other words, the Positive School wanted 'to assert scientifically and propose appropriate means in the need for a greater social defence against the criminals' offences' [di affermare scientificamente e di proporre i mezzi adatti nella necessità di una maggiore difesa sociale contro gli attacchi dei delinquenti] (Ferri 1883, p. 3).

The purpose of the repressive measures, thus, should be to guarantee the defence of society: crime being the symptom of a socially-dangerous behaviour, the security measures taken had to prevent further criminal activities by means of the removal of the criminal from society itself or of their medical treatment in a designated mental hospital.

3. Lombroso's Idea of Forensic Psychiatric Expertise

By determining the level of 'social danger' of the accused, and by providing credible evidence of their 'social responsibility' (Ferri 1892; Garofalo 1885), the Positive School—and then the Rocco Code—gave great importance both to the psychiatric evaluation of the defendant and to the role of the psychiatrist during the criminal proceedings.

According to Ferri, the following questions could be asked of criminal anthropology: 'Is the criminal always, or if not in what cases, a normal man or an abnormal one? And if and when he is abnormal, where does his abnormality come from? And is it innate or acquired? Is it correctable or not?' [Il delinquente è sempre, o in quali casi, un uomo normale o un uomo anormale? E se esso è e quando è anormale, onde proviene questa sua anormalità? Ed è essa congenita od acquisita, correggibile od incorreggibile?] (Lombroso et al. 1886, p. 74).

Lombroso was interested in the same matters when he explained very precisely what the forensic psychiatric expertise of the time consisted of in a little-known book entitled *La perizia psichiatrico-legale coi metodi per eseguirla e la casuistica penale classificata antropologicamente* [*Legal-Psychiatric Expertise with Methods for Conducting it and the Anthropologically-Classified Criminal Casuistry*] (Lombroso 1905). It was planned and written when Lombroso was 70 years old. At that period, he finally had a chair in criminal anthropology at the University of Turin and his theories and ideas were already widely used and recognized.

La perizia psichiatrico-legale is made up of two parts: the first collects many examples of criminal-anthropological evaluations, where every case-study described corresponds to a typology of mental disease, pathology or disorder; the second is more methodological, where Lombroso explains the tools and techniques to be used in a correctly performed anthropological and forensic-psychiatric evaluation.

In reality, many of Lombroso's books include famous examples of bio-anthropological and psychiatric evaluations (Frigessi et al. 2000; Lombroso and Bianchi 1884, 1905), but *La perizia psichiatrico-legale* is a practical testimony of how forensic psychiatric expertise was consolidated in those years and what was expected from it. It was, in fact, originally designed by Lombroso to be a handy guide capable of teaching the ways in which to carry out a psychiatric assessment when the Court requested it. The result is a catalogue including, on the one hand, numerous criminals' life stories and, on the other, the techniques used by nineteenth-century forensic psychiatrists in their evaluations.

By entering the medical history of the criminal, Lombroso simultaneously recommended the examining of their disease, their family surroundings (i.e., their social, economic, and 'cultural' circumstances) and, not least, their personality, temperament, and attitudes. Such a suggested method used to discover the criminal's behaviour comprised both a direct physical observation (i.e., concerning physical appearance and external factors) and an indirect one (i.e., laboratory tests). By means of anthropometric and cephalic measurements, anatomical and psychological examinations, emotionality, susceptibility and mobility testing, observations of tattoos, objects, pictures and papers written by the criminals themselves, and the analysis of interrogation reports, the psychiatric-legal evaluation was able to provide a biography of the accused and their bio-anthropological and psychological profile. In addition, Lombroso recommended the inclusion of an in-depth inquiry into their family, social, and 'cultural' background, as Salvatore Ottolenghi wrote in his *Programma di polizia scientifica per lo studio dei veri criminali* [*Scientific-Police Programme for Studying Real Criminals*]. Among other things, indeed, Ottolenghi suggested exploring the intelligence level (acculturation and education), individual skills, religious beliefs and practices, relationships (with family and friends), passions (political, patriotic, etc.), sexuality, morality (altruism, heroic acts, charity, honesty, loyalty, instincts of rebellion, etc.), the capability to commit crime (causes, manners, behaviours after crime), ideas of justice, remorse, recidivism, and so on (Ottolenghi 1910).

Although criminal anthropology was seen as a means for proving the link between the anomaly in the behaviour of the criminal and the (permanent or temporary) anomaly of their mind, it set out to study the two factors of human life as inseparable: the organic component and the psychic one together. Lombroso considered bio-anatomical examination so much as the very basis of psychic analysis that he specifically meant psychology as 'the study of the passions, the writings, the slang, the religion, the morality, the education, the mental illnesses, the historical, meteoric, hereditary, dietary influences behind the crime' [è lo studio delle passioni, degli scritti, del gergo, della religione, della morale, dell'educazione, delle malattie mentali, delle influenze storiche, meteoriche, ereditarie, alimentari sopra il delitto] (Lombroso et al. 1886, p. 44). However, he and his peers in anthropology had to prioritize the biological analysis because they believed 'the organ' needed to be studied before 'the function' that let it work.

Even if Lombroso did not explicitly speak about 'culture' or 'cultural conditionings', he did deal with elements, practices, and behaviours that could be qualified as 'cultural', secondary to physical causes and hereditary predispositions. His books and his forensic-psychiatric expertise are effectively based on reconstructions of criminals' lives: paradoxically, Lombroso used these qualitative analyses to provide an objective reconstruction of the criminals' lives in relation to their background, social environment, and adaptation to society.

Lombroso's tools and interpretations are controversial and obsolete, but clearly the focus of legal-psychiatric expertise is its presumed scientific method because it is believed capable of understanding the complexity that characterizes the criminal. He and his peers in psychiatry realized the importance of examining the criminal's life, relationships, and social and cultural background, while considering these only as circumstantial data to be used to provide an overall picture of the criminal. In order to learn more about their profile, Lombroso eventually highlighted the need for the input of all social and human sciences in the Italian penal system; nevertheless, he was repeatedly accused of treating the data merely as information rather than as a key resource for the understanding of the criminal.

Contrarily to the 'individualism' of the Classic School, indeed, the Positive School wanted to restore the equilibrium between the social element and the individual one (Ferri 1883). Demonstrating the abnormality of the criminal (as was required of legal-psychiatric expertise) thus meant evaluating both the suitability of the criminal for social life, and the degree of their anomaly, or better, as Garofalo (1885, p. 100) put it, 'if the anomaly is permanent and the mental illness is incurable or long-lasting in its dangerous form towards society, i.e., if there is any hope of improvement and suspension of the criminal impulses' [se l'anomalia sia permanete e l'infermità incurabile o duratura nella sua forma pericolosa alla società, ovvero se vi sia speranza di miglioramento e di cessazione degl'impulsi criminosi].

Forensic psychiatrists, therefore, were called both to deal with the criminal, biologically considered an anomalous subject because of their way of behaving, and to identify them in order to establish their degree of 'danger towards society'. This concept has its roots in one of Garofalo's intuitions, according to which the punishment should be determined on the basis of the 'fear' (i.e., the degree of insecurity) caused by the criminal towards society. For this reason, he proposed the distinction between the offence to social security and the probability of the crime's reiteration. It was Ferri then who recommended the use of the concept of 'danger to society' in order to differentiate the dangerous 'fact' from the dangerous 'man' (Ferri 1892; Garofalo 1885).

Since some criminal acts were interpreted as the results of mental disease, Lombroso believed most of them were affected by congenital mental anomalies, and therefore, were not to be considered responsible for their behaviours. Consequently, they had to be interned in special criminal psychiatric hospitals.

The Positive School concluded that the crime was 'an organic, psychic, and social abnormality' [il delitto è un'anormalità organica, psichica e sociale] (Lombroso et al. 1886, p. 104).

Even if faith in a positive science still persists in certain fields of behavioural genetics and forensic neurosciences as well as in some fields of psychology, psychiatry and criminology, most of the elements of Lombroso's bio-psychic anthropology are no longer accepted (Canepa 1974; Di Tullio 1931; Musumeci 2012). Italian cultural anthropology today, in particular, has expressly distanced itself from criminal anthropology. In Italy, 'criminal anthropology' actually coincides with Lombroso's criminal anthropology, because an anthropological field specifically dealing with 'crime' has not yet developed. Cultural anthropology inevitably rejected the biological and organicistic approach applied by Lombroso and the use he, and his peers in anthropology, made of the theories regarding the 'human race' (Lévi-Strauss 2002; Pogliano 2005; Stocking 1968). Moreover, the Nazi and fascist ideology decontextualized the evolutionary classifications of the human races produced by criminal anthropology and utilized them for justifying the 'scientifically-based' racial doctrine of segregation. By considering the debate on 'human race' a black page in Italian anthropology, cultural anthropology is thus reticent towards nineteenth-century (and particularly towards Lombroso's) Italian anthropology and rather it bases its approach on the understanding of cultural diversity. The hope is that Italian cultural anthropology will get more involved in studying the impact cultural diversity may have on the Italian juridical system, as well as on crime.

4. Psychiatric Expertise in Current Italian Criminal Trials

Among the various reforms proposed, the Positive School managed to shift the focus of penal law from the criminal fact, in the abstract, to the criminal individual, in concrete terms, and more specifically from the criminal's individual responsibility for the committed crime (as the Classic School affirmed) to their responsibility towards society (as argued by the Positive School). In order to determine their level of responsibility, Lombroso and 'his' School claimed to submit to the Court scientific, substantiated, objective and exhaustive expertise based on the biological origin of the criminal behaviour. The aim was to identify 'for sure', and so to prevent crime and to protect society from dangerous people.

If Lombroso underestimated the value of socio-cultural factors, Garofalo and Ferri improved the organicistic approach of their teacher by focusing the attention on the link between the individual behaviour of the criminal and their social background. When Garofalo (1885, p. 5) talked about 'social uses', i.e., 'the rules of behaviour to which most people are subjected' [norme di condotta a cui la maggioranza degli uomini si sottomettono], he sketched something similar to what we mean by 'culture' today. These rules, he continued (Garofalo 1885, p. 6), 'are there to guide almost every action of ours. Tradition, habit and example ensure that, without even investigating the reason, we are happy to submit to them and, in order to deserve the name of well-behaved people, we want to show in every occasion that we do not neglect them' [sono lì a dirigere quasi ogni nostro movimento. La tradizione, l'abitudine, l'esempio, fanno sì che noi, senza neppure indagarne la ragione, ci sottomettiamo ad esse volentieri, e per meritare il nome di persone ben educate, desideriamo mostrare in ogni occasione di non ignorarle].

The Positive School believed that violating social rules meant failing to adapt them. Indeed, its efforts focused not only on the practical norms establishing the different types of criminals, but also on the most appropriate penalty for every criminal typology.

Although Lombroso's classification of criminals has been surpassed, the Rocco Code pointed out the need for determining both the imputability (mental capacity) of the defendant and the danger of their act to society. The Code tried to find a compromise between the Positive School's proposals and the Classic School's philosophy: indeed, by introducing a 'double-track' system a Third School attempted to mediate between the idea of the free will and self-determination of the accused supported by the Classic School, and the factors conditioning human actions and behaviour referred to by the Positive School (Alimena 1900; Carnevale 1891).

That is why, even today, psychiatric forensic expertise is required for two kinds of assessments in criminal trials: the first to recognize the 'imputability' of the defendant, i.e., the causal link between their ability to understand and their will, and any kind of diseases that would exclude or diminish it. As maintained in article 85 of the Italian Penal Code, the 'ability to understand' is defined as the faculty to correctly comprehend reality (according to the values and principles expressed by society and relating to the stages and states of the life of the accused), while the 'ability to want' is defined as the ability of the accused to determine themself autonomously in the various circumstances of their life (Aleo and Di Nuovo 2011; Bertolino 1990; Ceretti and Merzagora 1994; Collica 2007; Dawan 2006; Monzani 2009). In addition, the Italian Penal Code indicates those cases in which the capacity to understand and take action excludes or diminishes mental capacity, such as mental illnesses (articles 88 and 89) or the consumption of alcohol or drugs (articles 91–95), a physiological immaturity due to minor age (articles 97 and 98) or a paraphysiological immaturity due to mutism and deafness (article 96). Conversely, emotional or passionate states are considered by Italian law not to exclude or diminish mental capacity (article 90).

The second kind of assessment demanded by expert psychiatric appraisal is to determine the dangerousness of the accused towards society in order to evaluate an alternative measure to imprisonment. As indicated in article 203 of the Italian Penal Code, dangerousness is defined as the probability that a defendant will commit a crime again. This article emphasizes the need to understand how the accused could be considered dangerous and what the risk level towards society is by means of a probabilistic evaluation (Caputo 2015; Dell'Osso 1985; Martini 2017; Pelissero 2008). The assessment of danger is oriented towards the future, and it is therefore indeterminate. For this reason, it needs to be integrated with all the elements pertaining to the 'personality', behaviour and background of the accused as indicated by article 133 of the Italian Penal Code.

By using a series of quantitative and qualitative parameters, these two kinds of technical response requested by the forensic psychiatric evaluation are presumed by the Italian criminal justice system to be capable of verifying both any mental disease related to the specific behaviour of the criminal and the chances that this could be risky for society (Aleo and Di Nuovo 2011; Ponti and Merzagora 1996). In this sense, the function of forensic psychiatry is to formulate an evaluation which is simultaneously diagnostic (imputability) and prognostic (danger to society).

Since forensic psychiatric expertise is a technical judgement, it is regulated by article 220 of the Italian Code of Criminal Procedure, and is considered to be a tool for obtaining information and means of proof at the same time. Experts are indeed requested to observe a very rigorous methodological procedure: after technical and legal preconditions, they have to proceed with the description of criminal facts, the collection of clinical data (and possibly historical data), the medical history, physical examinations and the laboratory and psycho-diagnostic tests in order to assess the mental capacity of the defendant, their capability to consciously participate in the trial, and their dangerousness towards society (Angelini and Verde 2010; Fornari 1997; Ingino and Scarfato 2016; Ponti and Merzagora 1996; Volterra 2005).

Even though this kind of forensic expertise includes collecting the accused's familial, social and interpersonal information, these data are intended to increase the information available about them, and not to be complementary to diagnostic and prognostic evaluations in any way. Consequently, their level of responsibility, guilt and maturity are still viewed as the essential result of scientific, objective and quantitative assessment rather than of the evaluation of cultural variables and conditions.

Current forensic psychiatric expertise in Italy appears unable to entirely assess the range of cultural differences—i.e., cross-cultural differences and the different kinds of social and cultural conditions and behaviours of the defendant—because cultural differences are not objectively quantifiable (Collica 2012; Merzagora 2017). At least three limitations for this can be noted: firstly, 'culture' cannot be considered as an entity, and its variety and variability are impossible to define objectively and universally; secondly, the tools and methods used to define the culture-related behaviours of the accused may be inadequate for giving evidence in Court; and finally, 'culture' does not appear as a key factor in the forensic evaluation of mental capacity, responsibility and dangerousness because it is considered closely associated to 'personality', i.e., concerning individual subjectivity, and thus the Italian Code of Criminal Procedure hinders its evaluation.

The key point here is that psychiatric expertise, as it is currently organized and planned, might be unable to take completely into account the complexity of human—and criminal—activity. Focusing on the criminal event (framed by time, place and situation), forensic psychiatry does not have all the tools for completely recognizing and revealing the complexity of circumstances that encouraged the criminal to commit the crime, especially when it is necessary to take into account appropriately every kind of culture-related manifestation of a particular disease. Effective support could come from the analytical tools of ethno-psychiatry and ethno-psychology. Basing their approach and appraisal on the recognition and respect of mutual cultural diversity, ethno-psychiatry and ethno-psychology reflect on the different culture-related psychic disorders and care systems developed in different cultural settings, thus questioning the belief in the presumed universality of both the 'Western' psychiatric categories of mental illness and the tools and techniques of the psychiatric science. In Italy, both disciplines—arising from the experiences gained within French ethno-psychiatry (Devereux 1978, 1980; Fanon 1952, 2011; Nathan 1986, 1993)—have recently been developing and refining their field of study and application, and they are trying to build a methodology capable of recognizing and treating the mental illness of members of diasporic communities (Beneduce 2007, 2010; Coppo 2003, 2007; Taliani and Vacchiano 2006). In this sense, they may effectively help 'official' forensic psychiatry because their approach aims at contextualizing, and filling with historical and cultural meanings, the traumatic (and potentially dangerous) experiences of immigrants.

From a legal viewpoint, the main strength of Italian psychiatric expertise (but also its biggest obstacle) arises from article 220 of the Code of Criminal Procedure, which states that expert appraisal is required when further investigation needs to be carried out and when the assessments need to specify technical, scientific or artistic competencies.

Indeed, if in the first paragraph article 220 closely correlates forensic expertise with technical and scientific competences, in the second it does not admit expertise concerning 'the psychological qualities independent of pathological causes'. This means that anything not having pathological causes (and therefore not to be based on technical and scientific evaluation), such as the accused's habits, skills, character, personality and customs, is left out of forensic expert appraisals.

Article 133 of the Italian Penal Code provides a possible alternative: according to this, the Judge has to 'deduce' the seriousness of the crime from a number of factors, among which include the nature, modalities, purposes, time and place, intensity and level of guilt of the crime. Furthermore, it indicates that the capacity of the accused to commit crime has to be 'deduced' from their reasons, character, criminal history, previous and concomitant conduct, and their living, individual, familial, and social conditions.

The critical point rests in the arbitrary nature of that 'deduction'. If the Judge does not consider themself able to comprehend the profile of the accused by means of using all the information obtained during the investigative work and in court proceedings, or they deem further assessment necessary, they may request a psychiatric evaluation by forensic consultants, which is the only instrument of evaluation they can use to understand the profile of the accused and to define an appropriate security measure for them. In practice, the Judge almost automatically requires forensic psychiatry to examine the defendant at the same time as the 'perpetrator' of the committed crime and as a 'potential perpetrator' of new crimes, in order to assess an appropriate social rehabilitation.

By making the close link between psychiatry and penal law increasingly vulnerable, this legal axiom appears fragile and leaves some doubts.

Firstly, in fact, mental illnesses are not the only causes of criminal acts. They may no longer be considered special causes of crime, but rather one of the many factors interacting with others in causing a criminal activity. This means that the social and cultural circumstances contributing to the crime do not inevitably have to be excluded *a priori* because current scientific tools are not able to evaluate them. For example, many social and human sciences, such as cultural anthropology, have developed and refined their methods and analytical tools in this sense. Already at the end of the nineteenth century, the Positive School emphasized the need to investigate the criminal as a whole with the contribution of all the social sciences.

Secondly, the accused's character, skills, customs and 'culture' are not simple corollaries of their criminal activity; rather, they are likely to form their background. In addtition, this inevitably also includes their behaviour: even though this is a controversial concept, in truth it does not reveal what the accused is, but rather what made the crime possible. By claiming their aim of the study (culture and its expressions), the anthropologists dealing with law and crime should clarify how 'culture' is debated in the Italian legal system in order to stress that culture not only is a concern of minority groups, immigrants or foreigners, but that it relates also to the anti-social behaviours of the majority of the population. The key matter, here, is how culture could be technically evaluated in order to provide an objective assessment. The Positive School has already answered this question, though only partially: considering the scientific competence behind its proposals, the Positive School, and Ferri (1892) in particular, recognized both the importance of introducing permanent social scientists in every court, and the need to teach criminal anthropology, biology, psychology, statistics and sociology to judges, magistrates and lawyers, in order for them to better understand the complex profile of each criminal and also crime as a social phenomenon.

Finally, objectiveness does not stand for science, but more likely for awareness techniques. Science bases its system of knowledge on using specific techniques able to provide a meticulous and understandable assessment because it guarantees both the impartiality of the consultant and the non-arbitrariness of evidence. In this perspective other sciences, like human and social sciences, may be equally qualified. Ferri (1883, p. 18), for instance, asked: 'But what reason would there be for denying social sciences that extension of the positive method which has already provided such great services in every other discipline?' He answered: 'Evidently none' [ma quale ragione vi sarebbe per negare alle scienze sociali quell'estensione del metodo positivo, che già rese così grandi servigi in ogni altra disciplina? Evidentemente nessuna]. The evaluations of cultural experts are expected to have the same objectivity, neutrality and validity as any other technical assessment in Italian legal proceedings. Since their expert testimony is the result of both a specific disciplinary training and suitable instruments used to understand and explain 'culture', anthropologists in Italy should also be seen as qualified consultants in criminal behaviours related to culture.

Indeed, the doubt raised by expert forensic psychiatric evaluations highlights the present-day need to work and refine tools of analysis capable of comprehending and interpreting cultural variables more than they do at present.

5. Against Discrimination: The Need for Cultural Experts

As all other competences, forensic psychiatry is based on the concept of impartiality. This relates to the objectivity of forensic consultants, and the neutrality of their assessment, which have to be valuable as evidence.

In Italy, however, such claimed impartiality was affected not only by the faith shown in positive science in the nineteenth century, but also by the racial classifications of human beings that culminated in the fascist ideology. This close link between science and race (Israel and Nastasi 1998; Maiocchi 1999; Manfredi 1988; Mantovani 2004) percolated into the Rocco Code too and still persists in Italian penal law in the fear of repeating that mistake again. The problem of analysing the 'personality' of the criminal arises from that very concern for categorizing people on the basis of assumptions, deductions and stereotypes as has happened in the past.

This difficulty mainly emerged at the end of the fascist period (when the concept of race was discussed by the intellectuals of the time) and in the 1970s, when waves of migration from outside Europe started to impact the Italian justice system.

The nineteenth-century Italian concept of culture corresponded to that of race. The race classificatory system was based on the study of human morphology and on the effort to find the biological, linguistic and historical origins of any race (Lombroso 1871; Mantegazza and Giglioli 1876; Niceforo 1901; Sergi 1900). The presumed scientific methods used to conduct that research, and the resulting categorizations of people, seemed to strengthen and justify the fascist ideology of nationalism and the superiority of the 'Latin race'.

Such a political view inevitably contaminated the Italian justice system too, and especially the Rocco Code which was drafted in that period. Not without reason, in the Second Book, Title Ten, the Rocco Code included 'Dei delitti contro l'integrità e la sanità della stirpe' [On Crimes Against the Integrity and Health of the Race], i.e., a number of articles (from 545 to 555) predisposed precisely for defending and securing an Italian national identity. Unlike the Zanardelli Code of 1889, the Rocco Code contained many culture-related articles which have now been revisited, deleted or repealed, such as those concerning the father's dominance over his sons and wife, the superiority of man over woman, public humiliation and shame, honour crimes, and so on.

In Italy, science in support of race was intended to promote the political and cultural identification of one nation with a single ethnic identity (Western and of Latin origins), a single religion (Catholic), a single language (Italian) and a single history, tradition, custom and culture.

However, even if most of the intellectuals and criminal lawyers of that time exalted Latin-ness, they strongly rejected the deterministic concept of race as biologically hereditary, and the eugenetic practices on which Nazi ideology was based because it was considered to be contrary to the Christian spirit (Mazzacane 1986; Pavan 2008).

Indeed, consisting of rejecting the research on the organic, biological and genetic origin of any race, while preserving the value of a common and single culture at the same time, that threat still persists in the Italian criminal justice system. Moreover, it was further impacted when migratory movements increased in Italy in the second half of the twentieth century.

During the Italian economic boom of the '1970s, immigration appeared as a social and legal problem. In the past, Italian immigration studies mainly concerned migratory movements from the South to the North of Italy—or beyond—for seeking employment. However, the impact of the diasporic communities moving around the world in more recent years has brought the concept of 'culture' into Italian trials as well. The historical, social, cultural and linguistic differences embodied by immigrants (and equally their economic inequalities) can make the understanding of their behaviours hard in the proceedings and increase the tension in the application of juridical norms.

Thus cultural expertise, and specifically the use of expert anthropological assessments as expert consultants of local law and conflict resolution, is an emerging need not only in the international context (Holden 2011, 2019) and specifically in the Italian justice system (Basile 2010; Bernardi 2010; De Maglie 2010; De Pasquali 2016; Gianaria and Mittone 2014; Ruggiu 2012). In Italy, indeed, social, human and criminal sciences question the legal effects deriving from cultural differences: such effects are difficult to comprehend, especially with reference to the resulting discriminatory and racist behaviours inside and outside the trials.

Since it might be seen as an opinion on what the criminal is and not on what they did, the Italian penal justice system excludes any kind of evaluation intending to reveal the personality of the criminal; it refuses any kind of expertise focusing on the biological origins of the mental illness or criminal behaviour of the accused, but explicitly requires the assessment of a specific event, i.e., the causal link between imputability and any potential mental disease that could preclude or diminish their capacity within the restricted time of committing a crime; it suggests a psychiatric assessment of dangerousness based on the future; and it limits any kind of culture-related evaluation, because of the complexity of defining the conditioning role of the cultural background on the behaviour of the accused and to avoid the risk of confusing 'culture' and 'race'.

Even though the concept of race—and the purity of race—has been overcome and scientifically denied, 'race' continues, however, to be a form of discrimination. The promotion of forensic assessments that seek to define the cultural identity of the accused in Italian trials is at risk of returning to racial or ethnic classifications. Yet the result of such a choice is often different types of discrimination (ethnic, racial, cultural, religious, social, economic, sexual, etc.), which is equally painful and unfair.

What is crucial, here, is again the concept of impartiality and the tools to be used for providing it. Reflecting on cultural expertise both as a technical tool and one of comprehension is a necessity nowadays in order to ensure the equality of any individual before the law. Together with other forensic sciences, cultural anthropology has to be considered as a valuable resource too, useful for understanding different cultural conditions and situations, and for making the mechanisms of cultural meetings or clashes clearer (Rosen 1977).

Based on the use of both technical and comprehensive tools, cultural competence aims to understand cultural differences and conditions in order to broaden their consideration and formulate strategies to let them live together. Anthropology, in particular, should also engage in the resolution of cultural conflicts in the Italian multicultural setting.

Cultural expertise, indeed, could be seen as something more than the mere interpretation of cultural differences: the technical evaluations, lines, and solutions offered by such anthropological competences may simultaneously explore criminal activity and behaviour related to the criminal as a person (their traditions, customs, social and familial situation, etc.) in order to facilitate their integration, rehabilitation and inclusiveness in society and to reduce discriminations and stereotypes in and out of the trial.

6. Conclusions

Traces of the rise and fall of psychiatric evaluation in Italian criminal proceedings, as well as the obstacles that limit the use of cultural expertise in this context have been documented in the history of the Rocco Code's drafting, between the end of the nineteenth and the first three decades of the twentieth century. Even though engaging cultural experts in Italy is an evident necessity, including anthropologists as consultants on the complexity of the criminal's profile is not a new idea. Criminal anthropologists of the late nineteenth century stimulated the legal system, proposed reforms and worked together with other social scientists to obtain an approved role in legal proceedings.

Although the current Italian penal system inextricably tries the imputability of the accused and the assessment of their dangerousness merely through the methods and tools offered by psychiatry, it reveals the need to obtain more information on their profile, background and manner of behaviour that may not always derive from investigative work, especially when cultural differences in behaviour, custom, law and language emerge and collide with criminal justice.

This 'grey zone' can be resolved by using tools specifically suitable for systematically revealing and comprehending the variety of cultural manifestations, and by investing in cultural expert assessments.

According to Ferri, the social factors of crime were among the most important achievements of the Positive School (Lombroso et al. 1886). The new School was already able both to show the capacity of social sciences to scientifically engage in the understanding of social—and 'cultural'—inequalities and to work on the requisites the criminal anthropologist should have had.

The limits for an effective use of anthropological knowledge in the Italian trial need to be better understood today: on the one hand, not all people have a complete knowledge of cultural anthropological competences (the recognition of the aim of cultural anthropology still causes many problems in Italy), while on the other some anthropologists are rather reticent if they have to deal with criminals and the criminal justice system. It would be necessary to inquire, therefore, how cultural anthropology in Italy is prepared to engage in legal proceedings and how it can work better together with the other sciences to achieve this aim (Ciccozzi and Decarli 2019).

Cultural experts (and cultural anthropologists first and foremost) can propose appropriate strategies by which to approach cultural differences and to determine the different cultural conditions of crimes without falling into biological classifications of criminals, stereotypes about race or arbitrary judgements of individual personality. Working on shared tools and guidelines, and on tested solutions, cultural experts may also provide information on the accused and their culture, which may bear value, credibility and impartiality so as to integrate expert psychiatric assessments. Not only, by helping psychiatric expertise improve its analysis and its data in a coherent and systematic manner, cultural experts may better define the imputability and dangerousness of the accused, which may help avoid cases decided on discriminatory grounds. Working on the cooperation between law and cultural anthropology, cultural expertise would prove itself very capable of providing efficient support for Courts when making decisions.

Funding: This research received no external funding.

Conflicts of Interest: The author declares no conflict of interest.

References

Aleo, Salvatore, and Santo Di Nuovo. 2011. *Responsabilità Penale e Complessità: Il Diritto Penale di Fronte alle altre Scienze Sociali: Colpevolezza, Imputabilità, Pericolosità Sociale*. Milano: Giuffrè.
Alimena, Bernardino. 1900. Lo studio del diritto penale nelle condizioni presenti del sapere. *Rivista di Diritto Penale e Sociologia Criminale* 1: 1–49.
Angelini, Francesca, and Alfredo Verde. 2010. *La Struttura Narrativa della Perizia Psichiatrica*. Milano: Ludes Press.
Baima Bollone, Pierluigi. 2003. *Dall'antropologia Criminale alla Criminologia*. Torino: G. Giappichelli Editore.
Basile, Fabio. 2010. *Immigrazione e reati Culturalmente Motivati: Il Diritto Penale nelle Società Multiculturali*. Milano: Giuffrè.
Beccaria, Cesare. 2001. *Dei Delitti e delle pene*. Milano: Fondazione Feltrinelli. First published 1764.
Beneduce, Roberto. 2007. *Etnopsichiatria. Sofferenza Mentale e Alterità fra Storia, Dominio e Cultura*. Roma: Carocci.
Beneduce, Roberto. 2010. *Archeologie del Trauma. Un'antropologia del Sottosuolo*. Roma-Bari: Laterza.
Bernardi, Bernardo. 1978. *Uomo, Cultura, Società: Introduzione agli Studi Etno-Antropologici*. Milano: FrancoAngeli.
Bernardi, Alessandro. 2010. *Il "Fattore Culturale" nel Sistema Penale*. Torino: G. Giappichelli Editore.
Bertolino, Marta. 1990. *L'imputabilità e il vizio di Mente nel Sistema Penale*. Milano: Giuffrè Editore.
Bulferetti, Luigi. 1975. *Cesare Lombroso*. Torino: Unione Tipografico-Editrice Torinese.
Canepa, Giacomo. 1974. *Personalità e Delinquenza: Problemi di Antropologia Criminale e di Antropologia Clinica*. Milano: A. Giuffrè.
Caputo, Alice. 2015. *La Pericolosità Sociale: Vecchie Esigenze e Nuove Prospettive alla luce della Legge 30 Maggio 2014, n. 81*. Roma: Aracne.
Carmignani, Giovanni. 1854. *Elementi di Diritto Criminale*. Napoli: Stabilimento Tip. P. Androsio.
Carnevale, Emanuele. 1891. Una terza scuola di diritto penale. *Rivista di Discipline Carcerarie* 21: 1–18.
Carrara, Francesco. 1867. *Programma del Corso di Diritto Criminale Dettato Nella R. Università di Pisa*. Lucca: Tip. Giusti.
Ceretti, Adolfo, and Isabella Merzagora. 1994. *Questioni sulla Imputabilità*. Padova: Cedam.
Chiarelli, Cosimo, and Walter Pasini. 2010. *Paolo Mantegazza e l'Evoluzionismo in Italia*. Firenze: Firenze University Press.

Ciccozzi, Antonello, and Giorgia Decarli. 2019. Cultural Expertise in Italian Courts: Contexts, Cases, and Issues. *Studies in Law, Politics, and Society* 78: 35–54.

Clemente, Pietro, and Fabio Mugnaini. 2001. *Oltre il Folklore: Tradizioni Popolari e Antropologia nella Società Contemporanea*. Roma: Carocci.

Clemente, Pietro, A. R. Leone, Sandra Puccini, C. Rossetti, Piergiorgio Solinas, and Pref. Alberto Mario Cirese. 1985. *Antropologia Italiana: Un Secolo di Storia*. Roma-Bari: Laterza.

Collica, Maria Teresa. 2007. *Vizio di Mente: Nozione, Accertamento e Prospettive*. Torino: G. Giappichelli.

Collica, Maria Teresa. 2012. La crisi del concetto di autore non imputabile 'pericoloso'. *Diritto Penale Contemporaneo* 1: 1–47.

Colombo, Giorgio. 2000. *La Scienza Infelice: Il Museo di Antropologia Criminale di Cesare Lombroso*. Torino: Bollati Boringhieri.

Comte, Auguste. 1831. *Cours de Philosophie Positive*. Paris: J. B. Bailliére et Fils.

Coppo, Piero. 2003. *Tra Psiche e Culture. Elementi di Etnopsichiatria*. Torino: Bollati Boringhieri.

Coppo, Piero. 2007. *Guaritori di Follia. Storie dall'altopiano Dogon*. Torino: Bollati Boringhieri.

Darwin, Charles Robert. 1859. *On the Origin of Species by Means of Natural Selection, or the Preservation of Favoured Races in the Struggle for Life*. London: John Murray Ed.

Dawan, Daniela. 2006. *I Nuovi Confini dell'imputabilità nel Processo Penale*. Milano: Giuffrè.

De Lauri, Antonio. 2010. *La Patria e la Scimmia: Il Dibattito sul Darwinismo in Italia dopo l'unità*. Milano: Biblion.

De Maglie, Cristina. 2010. *I Reati Culturalmente Motivati: Ideologie e Modelli Penali*. Pisa: ETS Edizioni.

De Pasquali, Paolo. 2016. *Criminologia Transculturale ed Etnopsichiatria Forense: Terrorismo, Immigrazione, reati Culturalmente Motivati*. Roma: Alpes Italia.

Dell'Osso, Giuseppe. 1985. *Capacità a Delinquere e Pericolosità Sociale*. Milano: Giuffrè.

Devereux, Georges. 1978. *Ethnopsychoanalysis: Psychoanalysis and Anthropology as Complementary Frames of References*. Berkeley: University of California Press.

Devereux, Georges. 1980. *Basic Problems of Ethnopsychiatry*. Chicago: Chicago University Press.

Di Tullio, Benigno. 1931. *Manuale di Antropologia e Psicologia Criminale Applicata alla Pedagogia Emendativa, alla Polizia ed al Diritto Penale e Penitenziario*. Roma: Anonima Romana Editoriale.

Fanon, Frantz. 1952. *Peau Noire Masques Blancs*. Paris: Editions du Seuil.

Fanon, Frantz. 2011. *Decolonizzare la Follia: Scritti Sulla Psichiatria Coloniale*. Verona: Ombre Corte.

Ferracuti, Stefano. 1996. Cesare Lombroso (1835–1907). *Journal of Forensic Psychiatry* 7: 130–49. [CrossRef]

Ferri, Enrico. 1878. *Teorica dell'imputabilità e Negazione del Libero Arbitrio*. Firenze: Barbera.

Ferri, Enrico. 1881. *I Nuovi Orizzonti del Diritto e della Procedura Penale*. Bologna: Nicola Zanichelli.

Ferri, Enrico. 1883. *La Scuola Positiva di Diritto Criminale. Prelezione al Corso di Diritto e Procedura Penale Nella R. Università di Siena Pronunciata il 18 Novembre 1882*. Siena: E. Torrini Ed.

Ferri, Enrico. 1892. *Sociologia Criminale*. Torino: Fratelli Bocca Ed.

Fornari, Ugo. 1997. *Trattato di Psichiatria Forense*. Torino: Utet.

Frigessi, Delia. 2003. *Cesare Lombroso*. Torino: G. Einaudi.

Frigessi, Delia, Ferruccio Giacanelli, and Luisa Mangoni. 2000. *Delitto, Genio, Follia. Scritti Scelti*. Torino: Bollati Boringhieri.

Garofalo, Raffaele. 1880. *Di un Criterio Positivo della Penalità*. Napoli: Leonardo Vallardi.

Garofalo, Raffaele. 1885. *Criminologia. Studio sul Delitto e sulla Teorica della Repressione*. Torino: Fratelli Bocca Ed.

Giacobini, Giacomo, and Gian Luigi Panattoni. 1983. *Il Darwinismo in Italia*. Torino: Utet.

Gianaria, Fulvio, and Alberto Mittone. 2014. *Culture alla Sbarra: Una Riflessione sui reati Multiculturali*. Torino: Einaudi.

Gibson, Mary, and Nicole Hahn Rafter. 2006. *Criminal Man*. Durham: Duke University Press.

Grottanelli, Vinigi. 1977. Ethnology and/or Cultural Anthropology in Italy: Traditions and Developments. *Current Anthropology* 18: 593–614. [CrossRef]

Holden, Livia. 2011. *Cultural Expertise and Litigation: Patterns, Conflicts, Narratives*. Abingdon: Routledge.

Holden, Livia. 2019. *Cultural Expertise and Socio-Legal Studies*. Special Issue. Bingley: Emerald.

Ingino, Nicoletta, and Riccardo Scarfato. 2016. *Colpevolezza, Imputabilità e Neuroscienze Cognitive: Criteri Giuridici e Conoscenze Scientifiche nella Valutazione della Responsabilità Penale*. Padova: Cleup.

Israel, Giorgio, and Pietro Nastasi. 1998. *Scienza e Razza nell'Italia Fascista*. Bologna: Il Mulino.

Knepper, Paul, and Per Jorgen Ystehede. 2013. *The Cesare Lombroso Handbook*. London: Routledge.

Lévi-Strauss, Claude. 2002. *Razza e Storia. Razza e Cultura*. Torino: Piccola Biblioteca Einaudi.

Lombardi Satriani, Luigi Maria. 1980. *Antropologia Culturale e Analisi della Cultura Subalterna*. Milano: Biblioteca Universale Rizzoli.
Lombroso, Cesare. 1872. *Genio e Follia*. Milano: Gaetano Brigola Editore. First published 1864.
Lombroso, Cesare. 1856. *Influenza della Civiltà su la Pazzia e della Pazzia su la Civiltà*. Milano: Tipografia e Libreria di Giuseppe Chiusi.
Lombroso, Cesare. 1870. *Studj Clinici ed Sperimentali sulla Natura, Causa e Terapia della Pellagra*. Milano: Tipografia di Giuseppe Bernardoni.
Lombroso, Cesare. 1871. *L'uomo Bianco e l'uomo di Colore. Letture sull'origine e la Varietà delle Razze Umane*. Padova: F. Sacchetto.
Lombroso, Cesare. 1876. *L'uomo Delinquente Studiato in Rapporto alla Antropologia, alla Medicina Legale ed alle Discipline Carcerarie*. Milano: Ulrico Hoepli.
Lombroso, Cesare. 1886. *Delitti di Libidine*. Torino: Fratelli Bocca Ed.
Lombroso, Cesare. 1888. *Palinsesti del Carcere. Raccolta Unicamente Destinata agli Uomini di Scienza*. Torino: Fratelli Bocca Ed.
Lombroso, Cesare. 1897. *L'uomo Delinquente in Rapporto all'antropologia, alla Giurisprudenza ed alla Psichiatria. Atlante*. Torino: Fratelli Bocca Ed.
Lombroso, Cesare. 1898. *In Calabria. Con Aggiunte del D.r. Giuseppe Pelaggi*. Catania: Niccolò Giannotta Editore.
Lombroso, Cesare. 1905. *La Perizia Psichiatrico-Legale coi Metodi per Eseguirla e la Casuistica Penale Classificata Antropologicamente*. Torino: Fratelli Bocca Ed.
Lombroso, Cesare. 1909. *Ricerche sui Fenomeni Ipnotici e Spiritici*. Torino: Unione Tipografica Editrice Torinese.
Lombroso, Gina. 1921. *Cesare Lombroso. Storia della vita e delle opere Narrata dalla Figlia*. Bologna: Zanichelli.
Lombroso, Cesare, and Augusto Guido Bianchi. 1884. *Misdea e la Nuova Scuola Penale*. Torino: Fratelli Bocca Ed.
Lombroso, Cesare, and Augusto Guido Bianchi. 1905. *Il caso di Alberto Olivo con Aggiunta in Appendice l'autobiografia di Alberto Olivo*. Milano: Libreria Editrice Nazionale.
Lombroso, Cesare, and Guglielmo Ferrero. 1893. *La donna Delinquente la Prostituta e la Donna Normale*. Torino: Editori R. Roux e C.
Lombroso, Cesare, Enrico Ferri, Raffaele Garofalo, and Giulio Fioretti. 1886. *Polemica in Difesa della Scuola Criminale Positiva*. Bologna: Nicola Zanichelli.
Lubbock, John. 1865. *Pre-Historic Times, as Illustrated by Ancient Remains, and the Manners and Customs of Modern Savages*. London: Williams and Norgate.
Lubbock, John. 1898. *The Origin of Civilisation and the Primitive Condition of Man*. New York: D. Appleton and Company.
Lucchini, Luigi. 1886. *I Semplicisti (Antropologi, Psicologi e Sociologi) del Diritto Penale: Saggio Critico*. Torino: Unione Tipografico-Editrice.
Maiocchi, Roberto. 1999. *Scienza italiana e Razzismo Fascista*. Firenze: La Nuova Italia.
Manfredi, Mario. 1988. Antropologia negativa tra Otto e Novecento. *Lares* 54: 5–48.
Mantegazza, Paolo. 1871. *Quadri della Natura Umana. Feste ed Ebbrezze*. Milano: Giuseppe Bernardoni, vol. I.
Mantegazza, Paolo. 1876. *Atlante della Espressione del Dolore*. Firenze: Giacomo Brogi Fotografo Ed.
Mantegazza, Paolo, and Enrico Giglioli. 1876. *L'uomo e gli Uomini. Lettera Etnologica*. Milano: Maisner & Co.
Mantovani, Claudia. 2004. *Rigenerare la Società: l'eugenetica in Italia dalle Origini Ottocentesche agli anni Trenta*. Catanzaro: Rubbettino.
Marotta, Gemma. 2004. *Teorie Criminologiche: da Beccaria al Postmoderno*. Milano: LED.
Martini, Adriano. 2017. *Essere Pericolosi: Giudizi Soggettivi e Misure Personali*. Torino: Giappichelli.
Mazzacane, Aldo. 1986. *I Giuristi e la crisi dello stato Liberale in Italia fra Otto e Novecento*. Napoli: Liguori.
Merzagora, Isabella. 2017. *Lo Straniero a Giudizio: Tra Psicologia e Diritto*. Milano: Cortina Raffaello.
Miletti, Marco Nicola. 2007. La follia nel processo. Alienisti e procedura penale nell'Italia postunitaria. *Acta Histriae* 15: 321–46.
Milicia, Maria Teresa. 2014. *Lombroso e il Brigante: Storia di un Cranio Conteso*. Roma: Salerno Editore.
Montaldo, Silvano, and Paolo Tappero. 2009. *Cesare Lombroso cento anni dopo*. Torino: Utet.
Monzani, Marco. 2009. *Imputabilità e Pericolosità Sociale: Un Binomio da Rivedere?* Napoli: ScriptaWeb.
Musumeci, Emilia. 2012. *Cesare Lombroso e le Neuroscienze: Un Parricidio Mancato: Devianza, Libero Arbitrio, Imputabilità tra Antiche Chimere ed Inediti Scenari*. Milano: FrancoAngeli.
Nathan, Tobie. 1986. *La folie des Autres: Traité d'ethnopsychiatrie Clinique*. Paris: Dunod.

Nathan, Tobie. 1993. *Fier de n'avoir ni pays ni ami . . . quelle sottise c'était. Principes d'ethnopsychanalyse.* Grenoble: La Pensée Sauvage.

Niceforo, Alfredo. 1901. *Italiani del Nord e Italiani del Sud.* Torino: Fratelli Bocca Ed.

Ottolenghi, Salvatore. 1910. *Trattato di Polizia Scientifica.* Milano: Società Editrice Libraria.

Pancaldi, Giuliano. 1983. *Darwin in Italia: Impresa Scientifica e Frontiere Culturali.* Bologna: Il Mulino.

Pavan, Ilaria. 2008. La cultura penale fascista e il dibattito sul razzismo (1930–1939). *Ventunesimo Secolo* 7: 45–78.

Pelissero, Marco. 2008. *Pericolosità Sociale e Doppio Binario: Vecchi e Nuovi modelli di Incapacitazione.* Torino: G. Giappichelli.

Pessina, Enrico. 1868. *Dei Progressi del Diritto Penale in Italia nel Secolo XIX.* Firenze: Stabilimento Civelli.

Pogliano, Claudio. 2005. *L'ossessione della Razza. Antropologia e Genetica nel XX Secolo.* Pisa: Edizioni della Normale.

Ponti, Gianluigi, and Isabella Merzagora. 1996. *Psichiatria e Giustizia.* Milano: Raffaello Cortina Editore.

Povolo, Claudio. 2007. Retoriche della devianza. Criminali, fuorilegge e devianti nella storia (ideologie, storia, diritto, letteratura, iconografia). *Acta Histriae* 15: 1–18.

Puccini, Sandra. 1991. *L'uomo e gli Uomini. Scritti di Antropologi Positivisti dell'Ottocento.* Roma: CISU.

Rosen, Lawrence. 1977. The Anthropologist as Expert Witness. *American Anthropologist* 79: 555–78. [CrossRef]

Ruggiu, Ilenia. 2012. *Il Giudice Antropologo: Costituzione e Tecniche di Composizione dei Conflitti Multiculturali.* Milano: FrancoAngeli.

Sergi, Giuseppe. 1900. *Specie e Varietà Umane. Saggio di una Sistematica Antropologica.* Torino: Fratelli Bocca Ed.

Sergi, Giuseppe. 1911. *L'uomo, Secondo le Origini, l'antichità, le Variazioni e la Distribuzione Geografica: Sistema Naturale di Classificazione.* Torino: Fratelli Bocca Ed.

Spencer, Herbert. 1879. *The Data of Ethics.* London: William and Norgate.

Stocking, George W. 1968. *Race, Culture and Evolution: Essays in the History of Anthropology.* Chicago and London: Chicago University Press.

Taliani, Simona, and Francesco Vacchiano. 2006. *Altri corpi. Antropologia ed Etnopsicologia della Migrazione.* Milano: Unicopli.

Tylor, Edward Burnett. 1871. *Primitive Culture: Researches into the Development of Mythology, Philosophy, Religion, Art, and Custom.* London: John Murray.

Velo Dalbrenta, Daniele. 2004. *La scienza Inquieta: Saggio sull'antropologia Criminale di Cesare Lombroso.* Padova: Cedam.

Villa, Renzo. 1985. *Il deviante e i suoi Segni: Lombroso e la Nascita dell'antropologia Criminale.* Milano: FrancoAngeli.

Volterra, Vittorio. 2005. *Psichiatria Forense, Criminologia ed etica Psichiatrica.* Milano: Elsevier Masson.

© 2019 by the author. Licensee MDPI, Basel, Switzerland. This article is an open access article distributed under the terms and conditions of the Creative Commons Attribution (CC BY) license (http://creativecommons.org/licenses/by/4.0/).

Article

The Cactus and the Anthropologist: The Evolution of Cultural Expertise on the Entheogenic Use of Peyote in the United States

Aurelien Bouayad

Law School, Sciences Po Paris, 27 rue Saint Guillaume, 75007 Paris, France; aurelien.bouayad@sciencespo.fr

Received: 16 April 2019; Accepted: 10 June 2019; Published: 17 June 2019

Abstract: This paper explores the complex evolution of the role anthropologists have played as cultural experts in the regulation of the entheogenic use of the peyote cactus throughout the 20th century. As experts of the "peyote cult", anthropologists provided testimonies and cultural expertise in the regulatory debates in American legislative and judiciary arenas in order to counterbalance the demonization and prohibition of the medicinal and sacramental use of peyote by Native Americans through state and federal legislations. In the meantime, anthropologists have encouraged Peyotists to form a pan-tribal religious institution as a way to secure legal protection of their practice; in 1918, the Native American Church (NAC) was incorporated in Oklahoma, with its articles explicitly referring to the sacramental use of peyote. Operating as cultural experts, anthropologists have therefore assisted jurists in their understanding of the cultural and religious significance of peyote, and have at the same time counseled Native Americans in their interaction with the legal system and in the formatting of their claims in appropriate legal terms. This complex legal controversy therefore provides ample material for a general exploration of the use, evolution, and impact of cultural expertise in the American legal system, and of the various forms this expertise can take, thereby contributing to the contemporary efforts at surveying and theorizing cultural expertise. Through an historical and descriptive approach, the analysis notably demonstrates that the role of anthropologists as cultural experts has been marked by a practical and substantive evolution throughout the 20th century, and should therefore not be restrictively understood in relation to expert witnessing before courts. Rather, this paper underlines the transformative and multifaceted nature of cultural expertise, and highlights the problematic duality of the position that the two "generations" of anthropologists involved in this controversy have experienced, navigating between a supposedly impartial position as experts, and an arguably biased engagement as advocates for Native American religious rights.

Keywords: cultural expertise; expert testimony; applied anthropology; controlled substances; peyote; entheogens; strategic litigation; indigenous rights; law and culture

---

1. Introduction

Since the earliest recognition of its use on Native American reservations in the late 1880s, peyote has laid at the heart of a series of legal battles over religious rights and indigenous self-determination in the United States (Stewart 1993; Maroukis 2012; Dawson 2018). Yet, in spite of the persistent assaults by the Bureau of Indian Affairs, Christian groups, physicians, and prohibitionist organizations in order to control, and ultimately eliminate, the psychoactive cactus in the interest of cultural assimilation, moral rectitude, religious purity, and public health, the entheogenic use of peyote has been able to survive both the prohibition and the war on drugs eras. Resulting from the confrontation of two radically different rationalities where the small hallucinogenic cactus constitutes either a narcotic or a sacred medicine, this long-standing and complex conflict finds its origin in the history of colonial

Mexico, and eventually became a reference point in the legal debate over nonrecreational use of psychoactive substances.

Drawing upon a socio-historical inquiry into this legal controversy, the article proposes a critical exploration of the evolution of the instrumental role that two generations of American anthropologists have played in this conflict as cultural experts (Grillo 2016; Holden 2011, 2019a, 2019b; Rodriguez 2018). Far from limiting themselves to expert witnessing, anthropologists have indeed proved strategic allies for Native Americans, counseling them in their interactions with the American legal system in order to protect their entheogenic practice from prohibition. This complex legal controversy, whose origins will be examined in Part 2, hence provides ample material for a general exploration of the use, forms, and impact of cultural expertise. Part 3 considers the role of anthropologists in assisting Native Americans in the defense of their entheogenic practice against early 20th century prohibition efforts. Led by James Mooney, anthropologists testified before lawmakers at several occasions, and later encouraged the movement's leaders to organize into an established church. Finally, Part 4 explores the reconfiguration of cultural expertise in the peyote controversy, as the proliferation of court cases after the Second World War led a new generation of anthropologists to provide strategic expert witnessing in defense of the peyote movement.

2. The Origins of the Peyote Controversy

Peyote (*Lophophora williamsii*) is a small and spineless cactus with psychoactive properties, which grows in a limited area situated at the junction of southern Texas and northern Mexico. It is light green and segmented, approximately one to two inches across, and grows singly or in clusters close to the ground from a long taproot. The plant is harvested by cutting off the exposed tops of the plant, leaving the root to produce more "buttons"—as the tops are usually called—which are then traditionally dried before being eaten. Despite its bitter taste, which usually causes unpleasant bodily symptoms—including nausea, dizziness, and vomiting—peyote is reported to produce a warm and delightful euphoria, relaxation, colorful visual distortions, stimulated imagination, and a sense of timelessness. The effects, caused primarily by the presence of mescaline—whose structure is partially homologous to LSD—peaks two to four hours after consumption, and declines over the next 8 h (Anderson 1996; Rojas-Aréchiga and Flores 2016).

The Aztec origin of the word "peyote" suggests that, for thousands of years before the "discovery" of America, populations living in the area of peyote growth along the lower Rio Grande and south into Mexico as far as Querétaro, were familiar with the plant and its psychoactive properties; recent archeological studies indicate that peyote is likely to have been known and used by native North Americans since at 5700 years ago (El-Seedi et al. 2005; Terrya et al. 2006). It can thus be assumed that the peyote cactus has been used for millennia as an entheogen[1] by American indigenous peoples and cherished for its curative properties, where it has been employed to treat such varied ailments as toothache, labor and breast pain, fever, skin diseases, rheumatism, diabetes, colds, and blindness (Schultes 1938). Although peyote has for a time been depicted by medical research as a dangerous drug in an effort to diabolize its use and justify prohibitionist efforts, it is nowadays generally recognized that the cactus is neither habit-forming nor harmful when used in the controlled ambience of a peyote ceremony (Halpern et al. 2005).

Although the use of peyote had been historically limited to indigenous peoples located in the territory of Mexico, prompting attempts by the Inquisition in New Spain to prohibit its use (Section 2.1),

---

[1] The neologism "entheogen" ("generating the divine within") refers to any psychoactive substance when used for its religious or spiritual effects, whether or not in a formal religious or traditional structure. This neologism, coined in the late 1970s by a group of ethnobotanists and religious scholars, including Richard Evans Schultes and Robert Gordon Wasson (Godlaski 2011), is often chosen to contrast with recreational use of the same substances. Entheogens have been used in a ritualized context for thousands of years and their religious significance is well established with anthropological and academic literature. Examples of traditional entheogens include psilocybin mushrooms, ayahuasca, iboga, salvia, and cannabis (Cavnar and Labate 2016).

the dynamics of colonial expansion in North America have resulted in the progressive diffusion of these entheogenic practices outside their traditional territory, all the way from Western Central Mexico to the Canadian province of Alberta (Section 2.2). This geographical expansion of peyote use, which led to the structuration of a vast religious movement in the United States, quickly became an object of interests for late 19th century anthropologists, and most notably for James Mooney, who played a crucial role as cultural expert in the defense of peyotism during the early 20th century (Section 2.3).

2.1. The Mexican Precedent

The Spanish, through the intermediary of missionary Bernardino de Sahagún, encountered peyote a couple of decades after their conquest of the Aztecs (León-Portilla 2002; Stewart 1993). To a large extent, they vigorously opposed the practice; not so much on account of its physiological effects, but because of its perceived religious significance for populations they were aiming at converting. Eating the peyote was declared by the padres to be almost as grave a sin as eating human flesh. The Inquisition in New Spain, established in 1571, consequently issued an edict of faith banning the use of peyote in June 1620 (Chuchiak 2012).

Following the publication of the edict, prosecution of cases related to the use of peyote ensued for much of the next two centuries, with a peak of repression from 1620 to 1650. Although the exact number of prosecutions related to peyote remains debated among scholars (Aguirre Beltrán 1963; Dawson 2016; Taylor 1996), the full force of the Inquisition's prohibition was to be felt on non-indigenous populations, firstly because of the controversial question of the Inquisition's jurisdiction of over indigenous peoples (Greenleaf 1965), but also because the risk of "contagion" was considered a more important issue than the continuation of heretical beliefs among the Natives (Quezada 1991). In any case, New Spain's colonial authorities did not succeed in eradicating entheogenic uses of peyote. After Spain lost control to Mexico in 1821, numerous evidence indeed indicate that peyote use was continued among tribes who lived in remote areas and where able to maintain their identities and traditions—most notably the Huichol, the Cora, and the Tarahumara, who continue until today to conduct elaborate pilgraimages to peyote fields (Lumholtz 1902; Benciolini and del Ángel 2016).

2.2. The Diffusion of Peyotism[2] in the United States

Although the use of peyote had been for a long time limited to populations located in the territory of what is now northern Mexico, the dynamics of colonial expansion in North America prompted the diffusion of these entheogenic practices outside of its traditional territory—to such extent that it would eventually become the first pan-tribal religion in the United States. Paradoxically, the federal policy of removing Native American tribes from their ancestral lands to newly created reservations in the 19th century played a critical role in the introduction of peyote in the country (Jahoda 1995). The situation of closeness induced by the massive relocation of these tribes, together with a shared condition of cultural disintegration, logically prompted exchanges among them, including the use of peyote in or near the newly established "Indian Territory"—which comprised present-day Oklahoma and parts of Arkansas.

The scale of the diffusion of peyote among fundamentally diverse Native American groups can therefore not be understood outside of this historical context. As the U.S. government was trying hard to suppress "backward cultures" through aggressive assimilationist policies—among which the Indian Religious Crimes Code, promulgated in 1883 (Irwin 1997)—new religious and spiritual movements emerged among native populations in order to find answers to this critical crisis of identity: these include the Ghost Dance movement and peyotism. Authors (Petrullo 1934;

---

[2] "Peyotism" generally refers to the entheogenic use of peyote as practiced by Native Americans; by extension, "peyotists" refers to the practitioners of the faith. The term was framed by Vincenzo Petrullo in his 1934 doctoral dissertation (Petrullo 1934).

La Barre 1938; Schultes 1938; Stewart 1993) have put forward other concurring factors in the further diffusion of peyote use: one of them is the role of the Carlisle Indian School, founded in Pennsylvania in 1879, and which remained the flagship Indian boarding school in the U.S. until 1918 (Adams 1997). Considering that over 10,000 Native American children from 140 tribes attended the school—many of whom became influential in tribal affairs when returning to the reservation—it is reasonable to assume that it helped the propagation of peyote use throughout the U.S. territory.

2.3. James Mooney (1861–1921) and the Early Ethnography of Peyotism

From the 1880s onward, with the availability of peyote, the development of railroads and the stability of life on the newly established reservations (Morgan and Stewart 1984), peyotism started to spread steadily beyond Oklahoma, thanks notably to the work of avowed missionaries such as that of Comanche Chief Quanah Parker (c. 1845–1911), who played a crucial role in the early structuration of the cult (Hagan 1993). The first description of a peyote ceremony was carried out by James Mooney in 1891, a few years after he was hired as an ethnologist by the Bureau of American Ethnology of the Smithsonian Institute (Colby 1978; Moses 2002). In 1890 and 1891, he traveled to Oklahoma in order to study the emerging Ghost Dance movement. He soon discovered that another religious movement was taking place in Indian Territory: the peyote religion—or, as he initially called it, the "mescal cult." Mooney managed to participate in several all-night peyote rituals; his notes and photographs are the first detailed description of the peyote ceremony in the United States. He wrote a number of relateed articles over the next decade, describing in detail the ritual and theology of the emerging religious movement (e.g., Mooney 1891, 1892, 1896).

The more Mooney studied the rite that had over time become a religion, the more he came to believe that the opposition to peyote by missionaries, Indian Service agents, and eventually reformers among Native Americans themselves was misdirected zeal. For the rest of his life, Mooney was much involved in studying the spiritual and medicinal rational behind the peyote cult. Convinced that peyotism was uniquely able to provide a source of unity and cultural integrity to the multitude of Native American tribes uprooted from their traditional territories and thrown together on reservations, he came to play a precursing and instrumental role as cultural expert in the legal defense of the entheogenic practice.

3. The Role of Anthropologists in the Legislative Battle Against Prohibition (1915–1937)

Peyotism thus gained progressive importance among Native American tribes throughout the end of the 19th and the early 20th century. However, in a context where psychoactive substances were becoming the targets of an emerging prohibitionist movement (Musto 1999), it was not long before missionaries and Indian Service agents became aware of the use of peyote, and tried by different legal means to stamp it out. Although Native Americans were for a time able to defeat repressive attempts on their own (Section 3.1), they soon realized that they would need the help of benevolent allies in order to prevent their opponents from passing prohibition statutes. Led by James Mooney, a first generation of anthropologists brought their help to Peyotists, providing testimonies before legislative bodies (Section 3.2), and later encouraged the movement's leaders to consolidate peyote use into an established religion whose practice would be protected by law (Section 3.3). The different modes of anthropologists' intervention during this first period of the controversy indicate that, beyond their role as cultural experts—which technically imply a neutral position—these scholars also became decisive advocates of this indigenous movement.

3.1. Early Regulatory Efforts

Closely connected with a passion to assimilate Native Americans, initial attempts to prohibit the use of peyote at the level of newly established reservations (Section 3.1.1) and Indian Territory (Section 3.1.2) did little to impede the spread of the movement. Peyote leaders even proved successful at defeating the passing of a state law in 1908, and skillfully argued the few cases that their devoted opponents were able to bring to court during this period (Section 3.1.3).

3.1.1. The Failure of Prohibiting Orders on Reservations

The first published reference to the use of peyote by Native Americans in the U.S. is credited to J. Lee Hall, agent of the Kiowa-Comanche Agency in the Indian Territory. In his 1886 annual report, he reported that "the Comanches and a few of the Kiowa secure the tops of a kind of cactus that comes from Mexico, which they eat, and it produces the same effect as opium. [...] suggest that the same should be made contraband" (Stewart 1993). This alert prompted initial regulatory responses by the Bureau of Indian Affairs (BIA) in the form of local executive orders aiming at prohibiting the practice at the level of reservations (Jackson and Galli 1977).

The first such order was issued by Special agent E. E. White of the Kiowa-Comanche Agency, on June 6, 1888. White then transmitted the order to the BIA, advocating for his initiative to be replicated in reservations where peyote had taken hold. The action was received favorably, and instructions were given to investigate the issue to all agencies and to prosecute the use, sale, exchange, gift, or introduction of the "mescal bean" as a misdemeanor under the rules governing the recently created Courts of Indian Offenses. The strategy however proved rather ineffective, as peyotism continued to spread in spite of the numerous prohibiting orders (Mooney 1897). White himself, less than two months after he posted the order, reached an agreement with the skillful Quanah Parker by which he permitted the Cheyenne "to use their [peyote] one night at each full moon for three or four months [...] and that they would not eat any at any other time. They also agreed that when their present supply of [peyote] gave out, they would quit entirely" (Stewart 1993).

3.1.2. The Inapplicability of the Territorial Law

Acknoweldging the shortcomings of prohibitive orders, the first statute to control the use of peyote was adopted in the Territory of Oklahoma in 1899. Declaring unlawful to introduce, possess, or sell any "mescal bean" on the Territory, the statute provided for a minimum punishment of twenty-five dollars and a prison sentence to a maximum of six months. Yet, reports by agents on reservation indicate that the law remained poorly enforced, as they were often confused and doubtful about how to do it (La Barre 1938). When it was finally tested in court in 1907, the statute was eventually astutely defeated by Peyotists thanks to the semantic confusion it carried.

Following a police raid of a peyote meeting on the information from a white farmer working with the Cheyenne and Arapaho, three Peyotists were arrested and charged for possession of "mescal beans." They were convicted by a probate judge on the basis of the 1899 Territorial law, and consequently fined twenty-five dollars each, and sentenced to five days in the county jail. On appeal, the District Court for the Kingfisher County however dismissed the case, holding that the defendants were found in possession not of mescal beans (*Sophora secundiflora*), but of peyote (*Lophora williamsii*); that the two were not the same thing; and that there was no law prohibiting the possession and use of peyote. Although seemingly trivial, this semantic confusion rendered the first legislative effort against the use of peyote in the inoperative[3].

---

[3] Another ceremony was raided in April of the same year in Custer County, Oklahoma, resulting on the arrest of nine Cheyenne and Arapaho Peyotists, and seven Native American "witnesses". The case was brought to trial at Arapaho in July, and a similar "semantic" defense was raised. Again, the court dismissed the charges, founding that mescal was not to be confused with peyote, and that the latter was not covered by the Territorial statute. Stewart reports that this semantic confusion dated back to the late 19th century, when the use of peyote was first observed by American authorities and confused with that of mescal (Stewart 1993).

3.1.3. An Attempt at Passing a State Law

At the turn of 1908, as Oklahoma was preparing to apply for statehood, local Indian Service agents who had been leading the charge on peyotism wanted to be ready for an anti-peyote state law, with the objective of setting a precedent to be replicated by other states where the religious movement was disseminating. As the time for the Constitutional Convention approached, promoters for the law sent support letters to members of the legislature and some even went to Guthrie to lobby members of the convention. Yet, Native Americans proved just as proactive in defending their interests. At the thirty-sixth day of the first Oklahoma legislature, over a hundred prominent representatives of the Comanche, Kiowa, Cheyenne, Osage, Ponca, Arapaho, Iowa, Sac, and Fox tribes filled the legislative hall. On four occasions, twice during the constitutional convention and twice at the first Oklahoma legislature six months later, Indian leaders assertively voiced their concerns about laws that restricted their rights to practice their medicine and religion (Wiedman 2012). On December 17, 1906, Quanah Parker was invited to speak before the Oklahoma constitutional convention, where he insisted on the medicial value of peyote use:

> Gentlemen, I am glad to meet you all this morning. My name is Quanah Parker. [...] I am an Indian myself; I am half white. My mother was a white woman; I attend to the government business for a good many years. [...] My Indians use what they call peotus; some call it mescal; all my Indian people use that for medicine. That is a good medicine and when my people are sick they use it. It is no poison and we want to keep that medicine. I use that and I use the white doctor's medicine, and my people use it too. I want to keep this medicine. I said while ago, my ways in time will wear out, and in time this medicine will wear out too. My people are citizens of the United States, and my people keep the right way; they go to school and teach school; I wish you delegates will look after my people—look after my Indians. (Oklahoma, Constitutional Convention 1907)

A month after his address, Parker returned from Guthrie with the assurance from President Murray and other delegates to the Constitutional Convention that no provision of the Oklahoma constitution will prevent the sale and eating of mescal beans (Wiedman 2012). The state law was thus eventually defeated, thanks to the ingenious adaptation of Native American leaders to the "white man's ways." However, prohibitionists did not disarm, and as efforts to ban peyote were gaining intensity with arrests, confiscation of property and verbal abuses on nearly every reservation (Dawson 2018), the need for new allies became urgent: hence emerged the first generation of anthropologists who, at various degrees, devoted themselves to the legal defense of peyotism.

3.2. The Increasing Involvement of Anthropologists in the Legislative Arena

By the end of the 1910s, peyotism had taken roots in at least eleven states beyond Oklahoma (La Barre 1938). This situation comforted opponents to peyote in the idea that comprehensive and concerted action was needed: they thus started to campaign actively for the adoption of a Federal law. Eleven bills were introduced in Congress between 1916 and 1937. All failed, however, thanks to the vigilance of Peyotists and the contribution of supportive anthropologists, who appeared several times before legislative bodies in order to testify as to the cultural significance of the practice for Native Americans. This was notably the case in 1915 before the Board of Indian Commissioners (Section 3.2.1) and during the pivotal 1918 House hearings (Section 3.2.2), providing early examples of the use of anthropological knowledge in Native American rights claims in the United States—three decades after the pioneer Choctaw Nation v. United States case (Gormley 1955). The same year, the intensification of prohibitionists' efforts led anthropologist James Mooney to encourage the movement's leaders to strategically incorporate into an establish church—a decision that would prove decisive in the evolution of the controversy.

3.2.1. Getting Prepared for the Federal Battle

In 1912, while the BIA sent out to all reservations Circular 598, which asked for information regarding diffusion of the practice, past court cases, and the "moral, mental, and physical effects" produced by the use of peyote, the Board of Indian Commissioners joined the lobbying efforts towards prohibition (Department of the Interior 1912). In February 1915, the Board called a session on the issue of peyote during its annual meeting, inviting interesting parties to testify as to the nature (and dangers) of the peyote cult. Alongside tribal leaders Otto Wells (Comanche), Arthur Bonnicastle (Osage) and tribal attorney Thomas L. Sloan (Osage), three anthropologists, members of the Bureau of American Ethnology, testified before the Board in defense of peyotism: James Mooney, Francis La Flesche[4], and Truman Michelson[5]. As opponents to peyote failed to attend the Board's hearing, the chairman of the meeting, Oklahoma Representative Charles D. Carter, was forced to admit that: "practically everything that had been said there by [anthropologists and Native Americans]—who were fine physical and mental specimens, to all appearances—[...] had been in favor of this religion and in favor of the plant itself, as the Indians use it". The board, however, issued a formal vote by which they opposed to the use of peyote in any of its forms, and in favor of legislation which will prevent Native Americans from obtaining it (U.S. Congress, House, and Committee on Indian Affairs 1918).

After a first attempt at amending the Indian Prohibition Law of 1897 by adding a mention to peyote was made in 1913—and eventually rejected by the Senate—similar propositions were made for three consecutive years; but never again did they pass neither the House nor the Senate (Maroukis 2012). Anti-Peyotists finally succeeded in introducing bills explicitly prohibiting the importation, transportation and sale of peyote before the U.S. Congress in 1916. The first bill (S. 3526) was however quickly defeated in Senate thanks to the commitment of Senator Robert L. Owen of Oklahoma, who responded to pressure from his Native American constituency. The next year, opposition to the Gandy Bill (H.R. 10669) was carried in person to Washington by a delegation of Native American Peyotists, who obtained a hearing on April 1916. Thanks to these concerted lobbying efforts, and because of the lack of scientific evidence backing anti-Peyotist arguments, the bill again failed to pass the House (Stewart 1993).

3.2.2. The Hayden Bill and the 1918 Congressional Hearings

Acknowledging the repeated shortcomings of the previous attempts, BIA requested in April 1917 Representative Carl Hayden of Arizona to introduce a new bill (H.R. 2614). This peyote prohibition bill, proposing punishments that would include a maximum of one year in jail and a $500 fine, constituted a pivotal moment in the peyote controversy, as both sides threw all their forces into the legislative battle. Extensive hearings were convened before a subcommittee of the House; taking place over six days and gathering no less than twenty-six testimonies, this moment thus provided one of the most dramatic examples of clashing political interests over the expression of Native American culture during the first part of the 20th century (U.S. Congress, House, and Committee on Indian Affairs 1918).

Missionaries and reformers led the opposition to peyote, substantiating the argumentation of the BIA—and trying to compensate for the rather inconclusive scientific evidence presented at the hearings. All of them denounced the dreadful and deleterious effects of peyote, and urged for its absolute prohibition, hoping that their call would resonate in Washington, where just months earlier the Senate had passed the Eighteenth Amendment. Zitkála-Šá, a member of the Yankton Dakota Sioux Tribe educated at Carlisle also known as Gertrude Bonnin and a fierce opponent to Peyotism

---

[4] La Flesche (1857–1932) was born on the Omaha reservation in Nebraska, and became the first professional Native American anthropologist. He joined the Bureau of American Ethnology in 1910, and remained until his death. He investigated the practice of peyote use among the Ponca and the Osage, although he did not published significant work about peyotism (Mark 1982).

[5] Michelson (1879–1938) a distinguished linguist, was not as experienced as Mooney and La Flesche in relation with peyote, but had the occasion to observe ceremonies among the Northern Arapaho in Wyoming (Boas 1938).

(Lewandowski 2016), gave a perfect summary of the prohibitionists' rationales, reciting the evils of peyote:

> Believing that peyote is the comforter sent by God, they reject the teachings of the Church. Believing that peyote reveals the secret thoughts of man and gives super human knowledge of the contents of books, they deprecate the necessity of schools. Believing peyote a cure-all for every human ailment, they ignore the advice and aid of physicians. Attending the weekly peyote meetings, they waste time, strength, and money, consequently neglecting their homes and farms. (U.S. Congress, House, and Committee on Indian Affairs 1918 [emphasis added])

In defense of their entheogenic practice, ten Native American representatives provided statements at the hearings, trying to convince the subcommittee of the innocuousness and the religious sincerity of their use of peyote. Beside them, the three anthropologists who already testified at the 1915 session—as well as the already prominent ethnobotanist William Safford—provided a rich expertise in support of the movement. Leading the way, James Mooney intervened at length during the hearings. He gave a detailed history of Peyotism and the reason for its rapid and steady spread beyond traditional tribal barriers, and provided a handful of arguments to counteract prohibitionists' alarming statements—pointing notably at the poor quality of the available scientific data on peyote and on its effects. Michelson's and La Flesche's testimonies were relatively less substantive, as they had considerably less experience and knowledge about Peyotism. However, based on their observations among the Arapaho for the former, and the Ponca and Osage for the latter, they affirmed that they were thoroughly convinced by the religious sincerity of those who participated in the cult, and insisted on the grave consequences that its suppression would induce. This mode of legislative intervention was evidently crucial, allowing cultural experts to document and demonstrate the cultural depth of Peyotists' entheogenic practice before federal lawmakers.

Mooney however received a particularly hostile reception. His lengthy defense of the medicinal and religious significance of peyote was repeatedly met with hostility—if not disdain—by members of the subcommittee. General Richard H. Pratt went even further, challenging the impartiality of the anthropologists' statements: accusing them of encouraging Native Americans to maintain "old, unhealthy, and uncivilized customs" so they could continue writing exotic books, and thus exploit Native Americans while doing nothing to help them become civilized; the former head of the Carlisle Indian School directly questioned Mooney's probity and made several insinuations about the role of anthropologists in the spread of Peyotism:

> My experience is that the Bureau of Ethnology has never been helpful to the Indians in any respect [...] the ethnologists always lead the Indian's mind back into the past. [...] You ethnologists egg on, frequent, illustrate, and exaggerate at the public expense, and so give the Indian race and their civilization a black eye in the public esteem. It was well established at the time of the ghost-dance craze among the Indians that white men were its promoters if not its originators. That this peyote craze is under the same impulse is evident from what appears in this evidence. (U.S. Congress, House, and Committee on Indian Affairs 1918)

Beyond the caricature nature of General Pratt's attacks, the general dismissal of Mooney's argumentation at the hearings heuristically underlines the problematic duality of the anthropologists' position in this legal controversy, navigating between a supposedly impartial position as cultural experts, and an arguably biased engagement as advocates for Peyotists' religious rights. It should be further noted that Pratt's assertions resonate to a certain extent with the critics against anthropology's tendency for paternalist primitivism that emerged from within the discipline since the 1960s (e.g., Foster 1969; Lewis 1973; Memmi and Greenfield 1967).

Mooney endeavored to respond to these accusations. He claimed—in a no less simplistic manner—"Now, in regard to an ethnologist never having helped the Indians. As a matter of fact, anybody who knows anything about ethnologists knows that is not true. The Indians look up on ethnologists as their best friends." In any case, Pratt's rhetorical strategy undoubtedly suggests that anti-Peyotists had come to acknowledge the crucial role of anthropologists' testimony for the legal defense of the entheogenic practice they were trying to stamp out. In its report in favor of prohibition submitted after the 1918 hearings, the House subcommittee hence made a particularly interesting claim on this matter, implicitly supporting Pratt's attacks on Mooney as untrustworthy and self-interested:

> The proof is clear that the physicians, the chemists, the missionaries, and many of those who are endeavoring to uplift the Indian, are convinced of the harmful effects of peyote and desire to see its use discontinued. [...] The writer of this report heard many Indians testify on behalf of the drug, and gave due weight to their testimony, but certainly they are to some extent interested, while the bulk of those advocating the passage of the bill are disinterested. (U.S. Congress, House, and Committee on Indian Affairs 1918 [emphasis added])

This was however not enough to secure the adoption of prohibitory legislation. The bill passed the House on October 3, 1919, but was rejected in the Senate, thanks again to the efforts of Oklahoma Senator Robert L. Owen (Owen claimed Cherokee ancestry and had been a teacher and Indian Agent among the Cherokee earlier in his career); arguing that the ban represented a violation of Native American First Amendment rights and managed to quash the bill (Belcher 1953); thus ending the most serious attempt to pass a federal law: explicitly prohibiting the use of peyote.

3.3. The Creation of the Native American Church

The legislative battle of 1918 constituted a particularly tough fight, and Peyotists realized that they won a close victory. Aware that the battle was not over, James Mooney and several of the movement's leaders understood that in order to prevail again, they would have to find a way to consolidate the legality of peyote use. Hence emerged the idea to make Peyotism conform to other religious institutions, and to equate the ceremonial use of peyote to the sacramental use of wine by Catholics and Jews—which had just received constitutional protection in the context of the prohibition (Newsom 2005). But to be recognized as a religious organization, Peyotists needed more than their personal belief: they needed a name, a set of rules, officers, and stated responsibilities. They needed to be "incorporated." With several state bans already in place (see infra Section 4.1.1) and a national ban narrowly avoided, the leading Oklahoma Peyotists therefore gathered in the end of the summer of 1918 in El Reno to draw up a charter and establish a peyote church.

3.3.1. A Preventive Legal Strategy

Assembling the representatives of most Native American tribes in Oklahoma, for whom the 1918 hearings had become a springboard to action, the group did not equivocate about the use of the word peyote, realizing that this was the issue and that it had to be openly acknowledged. The Article 2 of the Native American Church (NAC) Certificate of Incorporation, signed on October 10, 1918, thus read,

> The purpose for which this corporation is formed is to foster and promote the religious belief of the several tribes of Indians in the state of Oklahoma, in the Christian religion with the practice of the Peyote Sacrament as commonly understood and used among the adherents of this religion. (Stewart 1993 [emphasis added])

The decision to incorporate a peyote church, whose name emphasized both the Christian and indigenous roots of the church, as well as its pan-tribal nature, would soon prove instrumental in preventing a total federal ban on peyote. Not only did it place Peyotists within the established legal architecture, thereby allowing them a floor from which to debate, but it also gave them strength in numbers[6].

---

[6] The NAC nowadays claims close to 300,000 members and hundreds of local chapters, with members belonging to more than seventy Native American tribes. The church has retained a complex and loosely organized structure, divided between four

The incorporation of the church was vigorously and consistently denounced by opponents to peyote as an opportunistic strategy (e.g. Bureau of Indian Affairs 1922). Yet, the sincerity of the religious dimension of the ceremony for Native American users of peyote was never seriously challenged in court or before legislative and administrative authorities. This strategy of preventive legal action therefore constitutes a remarkable case of cultural adaptation of Native Americans to the "colonizers' mentality": it demonstrates a profound understanding of the role of legal institutions in the U.S. and of how Native Americans could adapt to the political system that was being imposed upon them in order to effectively safeguard their ritual practice against relentless opponents. Only a few decades after the end of the Indian Wars, this episode indicates that the "civilization of the Indian" had yielded unforeseen results.

3.3.2. The Role of Anthropologists in the Creation of the NAC

The implication of James Mooney in the incorporation of the NAC certainly constitutes a unique example of anthropologists' involvement in indigenous rights controversies, particularly with respect to the modality of its intervention as cultural expert (Holden 2019b). In this instance, Mooney's role has indeed not consisted in delivering expert testimonies for the use of courts or legislative bodies, i.e., in translating in legally legible terms an exotic culture in the context of legal proceedings, but rather in assisting an indigenous community in its strategic adaptation to, and recapture of the cultural patterns of the majority group. Although we lack precise information, several sources suggest that Mooney, alongside tribal lawyers, played an instrumental role in the Peyotists' decision of establishing the NAC, recognizing that making explicit the sacramental nature of the peyote ceremony in the articles of incorporation would help consolidate the religious character of the movement, and thereby significantly complicate the legal crusade of anti-Peyotists.

According to Maroukis (2012) and Moses (1978), Mooney returned to Oklahoma after the congressional hearings in early July 1918, fearing that the Hayden bill would eventually be adopted. He visited many of his Native American friends and informers, attended peyote services, and several elements suggest that he played a crucial role in the foundational meeting of El Reno. According the testimony of Kiowa-Apache Jim Whitewolf, Mooney was present at the meeting, and even recommended the name "Native American Church," despite the overwhelming presence of Oklahoma Peyotists. Slotkin similarly reported in its 1955 work on the sociology of the peyote movement that there was "reason to believe that it was on Mooney's initiative that the Native American Church was incorporated in Oklahoma" (Slotkin 1955).

The implication of Mooney in the institutional consolidation of Native American Peyotism constitutes a remarkable illustration of anthropologists' dilemma when, called upon to provide neutral and independent expertise for legal purposes, they sometimes find themselves invested in parallel advocacy practices in support of minority rights that tend to question their impartiality—or even their academic credibility. This debate over cultural experts' neutrality, which later unfold primarily in relation to anthropologists' expert witnessing per se (Rosen 1977; Lewis 1988; Mertz 1994), has proved a complex question in consideration of anthropologists' frequent engagement towards the protection of subaltern and vulnerable groups, raising ethical and deontological issues beyond legal and political considerations. In the case of Mooney, whether or not he actually participated in the drafting of the NAC articles of incorporation, it remains that members of the Indian Service administration were convinced that he had counseled and supported the officers of the newly created church.

---

main branches—none of which having any direct theological or legal control over the others—: the NAC of Oklahoma, the NAC of North America, the Azee Bee Nahagha of Diné Nation, and the NAC of South Dakota (Smith and Snake 1996; Maroukis 2012).

3.3.3. The Subsequent Retaliation against James Mooney

This suspicion had direct and dire consequences on the career of Mooney. His return to Oklahoma in July 1918, only a few months after the heated hearings before the House subcommittee, further aggravated the exasperation concerning its implication in defense of Peyotism. Informed of the situation by Agency officials and missionaries, Indian Commissioner Cato Sells requested the director of the Smithsonian Institution to take immediate action. He explained to Secretary Walcott: "I regard the situation [...] as a serious interference with our efforts to control and eventually entirely eliminate the use of peyote by Indians and feel that you will appreciate the advisability of the immediate recall of Mr. Mooney" (Moses 1978). The Bureau of American Ethnology endeavored to resist governmental pressure, putting forward Mooney's reputation—notably in relation to his foundational work on the Ghost Dance movement (Mooney 2012). Yet, he was eventually recalled and never again allowed to return to Oklahoma to continue his study. By 1921, Mooney was severely ill, and his salary at the Bureau of American Ethnology slashed for "nonproduction." In a letter he wrote to a colleague in Oklahoma just before he left the service that September, Mooney lamented that the government was looking for opportunities to "impede and suppress" his peyote investigations "altogether, to leave the way clear for hostile legislation" (Dawson 2018). James Mooney died a few weeks later of a heart attack.

This episode of institutional retaliation demonstrates the distress of prohibitionists, and dramatically speaks for the crucial role that James Mooney played throughout this period. At the end of the 1910s, Native American Peyotists, with the help of supportive anthropologists who both testified before legislative bodies and put their knowledge of the American legal system at the service of the movement, had won two crucial battles with the very weapons of their opponents.

4. The Role of Anthropologists in the Legal Defense of Peyotism before Courts (1956–1980)

The failure of the Hayden bill and the opportunistic incorporation of the Native American Church that followed led advocates of a federal prohibition to a deadlock. Anti-Peyotists continued to introduce new bills almost every year from 1919 to 1926—without success. They thus shifted their efforts to state legislatures, where they were able to secure the adoption of anti-peyote laws in two-dozen states (Section 4.1). Peyotists were consequently forced to adapt their legal strategy, and started to embrace a test case approach after the Second World War in order to challenge the constitutionality of these new laws before courts. They were helped in this by a new generation of anthropologists who further developed the academic understanding of the peyote movement beyond Mooney's pioneer research and adopted a new mode of legal intervention: expert witnessing (Section 4.2).

However, this reconfiguration of the controversy, and the substance and modality of anthropologists' involvement, allowed for an essentialist narrative of Peyotism to progressively consolidate. This evolution—conforming the entheogenic practice to a broadly conceived version of indigeneity and long-standing orientalist views of the "mystical Indian"—played a critical role in the protection of the use of peyote by Native Americans. The psychoactive cactus became an Indian thing, beyond the comprehension of the white man, something that could form the basis of a religion exclusive to indigenous peoples. This strategic essentialization of Peyotism, despite its ethnographic simplification, ultimately provided the basis for subsequent claims of legal exemptions, at a moment where the U.S. were preparing to embark on an all-encompassing policy of drug prohibition.

4.1. The Reconfiguration of the Peyote Controversy

4.1.1. The Multiplication of Anti-peyote State Laws; and Their Relative Efficiency

The national campaign against peyote, which proved eventually ineffective at the federal level, met with more success in state legislatures where Oklahoma Peyotists had limited—if any—lobbying capacity. A year before the 1918 hearings, prohibitionists were thus able to pass anti-peyote statutes in three states: Utah, Colorado, and Nevada. Many more were to follow.

In Utah, the legislative effort was driven by Gertrude Bonnin; already a veteran fighter against Peyotism, she was then living on the Ute reservation, where peyote had been introduced a few years earlier, and had already been adopted by nearly half of the reservation. Alarmed by the situation, she reached to the state Governor, calling for his help. She substantiated her request with the testimony of the reservation's physician, Dr. Henry Lloyd, who denounced the fatal consequences of peyote use and called its religious dimension "a travesty." His testimony perfectly exemplifies the rationale behind its profession's radical opposition to peyote, viewed as a dangerous concurrent to the White man's medicine (Welsh 1918). The first state law prohibiting the possession and use of peyote was thus prepared, and eventually adopted in February 1917[7]. Kansas became the fourth state to outlaw peyote in 1919, followed in 1923 by Arizona, Montana, and North and South Dakota. Iowa, New Mexico and Wyoming, and Idaho passed similar laws (in 1925, 1929, and 1933, respectively). Hence, at the notable exception of Oklahoma—where the cult emerged—and Texas—where peyote grew and was collected and shipped across the national territory—almost every Western States concerned with the use of peyote at that time had adopted prohibitive regulations by the early 1930s.

State laws however proved largely futile in impeding the spread of Peyotism. This was largely the consequence of the limited jurisdiction of state courts: as long as Native Americans practiced peyote on their reservations, and in the absence of federal or tribal law prohibiting it, they were free to do so. States could therefore only interfere with the interstate trade of peyote, although this was largely circumvented by Peyotists directly traveling to Oklahoma and Texas in order to bring back peyote themselves, and by the concrete difficulty of such a control (Stewart 1993). Furthermore, local Indian Service agencies and the BIA in general were significantly more concerned and invested in the rampant alcohol traffic and its devastating effects on Native American populations (Martin 2003; Antell and Holmes 2001).

4.1.2. Following the Trail of James Mooney

Meanwhile, a new generation of anthropologists born in the early 20th century progressively emerged to continue and broaden the seminal work of James Mooney—and, to a lesser extent, of Alfred Kroeber[8]. All of them carried out their fieldwork among different Native American tribes in the 1930s and early 1940s, and although most were interrupted by the Second World War, they all published influential works on Peyotism, providing a rich source of documentation and argumentation that allowed for the legal defense of the practice before courts (Section 4.2).

Among them was Weston La Barre (1911–1996). Born in Uniontown (PA), he studied at Princeton and Yale, and later taught at Rutgers, Wisconsin, and Duke Universities. "The Peyote Cult", La Barre's doctoral dissertation presented at Yale University in 1937, was the result of two summers of fieldwork he conducted in 1935 and 1936 among the Kiowa. The manuscript, based on a plethoric bibliography, was published in 1938, and immediately became the reference source on the peyote movement—notably as James Mooney was not able to carry such work (Moses 2002). Alongside La Barre was ethnobotanist Richard Evans Schultes (1915–2001), who accompanied him in his second fieldtrip while he was working on his undergraduate senior thesis in biology. Schultes later published "The Appeal of Peyote", a provocative article in which he claimed that the diffusion of peyote should

---

[7] Gertrude Bonnin also participated in the legislative effort in Colorado and Nevada, where anti-peyote statutes were enacted simultaneously in February 1917. In the case of Nevada, it is interesting to note that the prohibition was adopted a by the mid-1930s was organized on fourteen reservations and had well over ten-thousand members, decades before peyotism actually started to spread in the state (Stewart 1993).

[8] Alfred L. Kroeber (1876–1960), a figure of American cultural anthropology, received his Ph.D. under the supervision of Franz Boas at Columbia University in 1901 (the first doctorate in anthropology awarded by the University). He then became the first professor appointed to the Department of Anthropology at Berkeley University. He observed and wrote about the use of peyote in the context of his doctoral research among the Arapaho (Kroeber 1902).

be understood in relation to the medicinal value that Native Americans attribute to it, rather than to its spiritual significance (Schultes 1938)[9].

The first monograph on Peyotism was however published in 1934 by Vincenzo Petrullo (1906–1991): titled "The Diabolic Root: A Study of Peyotism, the New Religion Among the Delawares", it was result of the Ph.D. in Anthropology he obtained at the University of Pennsylvania the same year (Petrullo 1934). The contribution of James Slotkin, although published later, also deserves to be evoked here. Receiving his Ph.D. in Anthropology from the University of Chicago in 1940, Slotkin (1913–1958) published in 1952 the results of his research on Menominee Peyotism with ethnomusicologist David P. McAllester (Slotkin and McAllester 1952). He also produced groundbreaking research on the historical origins of the movement (Slotkin 1951, 1955). Finally, he published the reference work on the early history of the Native American Church (Slotkin 1956). In 1954, he was nominated on the board of trustees of the NAC, and brought his help in furthering the organization of the Church; he notably introduced printed membership cards and certificates of group affiliation for members in order to strengthen legal protection. Working closely with NAC President Dale, Slotkin also offered to publish a quarterly newsletter for the NAC and to distribute and analyze a questionnaire to document the location and number of NAC members (Stewart 1993).

Last but not least was Omer C. Stewart (1908–1991). Trained in anthropology at the University of Utah and the University of California at Berkeley, where he carried out his fieldwork on southwestern tribes' Peyotism and received a doctorate in 1939, Stewart published close to thirty articles and monographs on the topic (e.g., Stewart 1941, 1944, 1948; Aberle and Stewart 1957), together with a crucial book on the origin and spread of the peyote movement (Stewart 1993). In this connection, he was appointed as expert witness in eight court cases from 1960 to 1982, where he vehemently defended the right of Native Americans to use peyote as a sacrament. Just as James Mooney proved instrumental in the legal incorporation of the NAC and the correlated efforts to block the passing of federal laws against peyote during the early 20th century, Stewart was undoubtedly a fundamental asset in the legal strategy elaborated by the NAC to fight state prohibition laws.

4.1.3. The Evolution of the Federal Attitude Towards Peyote

However, before exploring this "second period" of anthropologists' involvement with the legal defense of Peyotism, a few words should be said about the establishment of a tolerant federal attitude towards the movement. Indeed, in the midst of the Great Depression, the election of Franklin D. Roosevelt in 1932 not only brought a "New Deal" to the American people generally, but also prompted what was later framed as the "Indian New Deal," which (notably with the Indian Reorganization Act of 1934) aimed at reversing the long-standing policy of cultural assimilation of Native Americans.

John Collier, a noted Native American rights advocate and former executive secretary of the American Indian Defense Association who in the early 1920s had the opportunity to witness in person the spread of the peyote religion among the Navajo, was sworn in as Indian Commissioner on April 1933. Together with Secretary of Interior Harold L. Ickes, he brought a new philosophy to the Bureau of Indian Affairs, with a radical departure from the idea that the purpose of the Bureau was to encourage Native Americans to forego everything Indian as soon as possible and strive to assimilate. Feeling that the very presence of Indian culture was a great asset to American society, he considered that "the government should reawaken in the soul of the Indian not only pride in being an Indian, but hope for the future as an Indian. It had the obligation to preserve the Indian's love and ardor toward the rich values of Indian life as expressed in their arts, rituals, and cooperative institutions" (Philip 1977). This new philosophy of Indian affairs led to an evolution of the federal attitude toward the peyote issue, which was expressed in the Bureau Circular 2970 of 1934. Entitled Indian Religious freedom and Indian

---

[9] Schultes's argument was challenged by La Barre, who succeeded in imposing his view that the "religious appeal" of peyote was the crucial element behind peyotism's rapid and vast expansion (La Barre 1939).

Culture, it stated that "no interference with Indian religious life or ceremonial expression will hereafter be tolerated" (Prucha 1990). This profound shift, reflecting Collier's emphasis on Native American self-determination, constitutes the first policy statement specifically intended at protecting Native American religious rights, and allowed putting the entheogenic use of peyote out of prohibitionists' reach at the federal level for several decades (O'Brien 1995).

Yet, this reorientation of the federal Indian policy also undeniably participated in the consolidation of an essentialist approach towards Native American cultural and religious expressions (Rosemblatt 2018)—including de facto peyote use. This evolution, eventually reflected in the practical and substantive transformation of anthropologists' involvement in the controversy during this period, found its first concrete illustration in 1937, after a new anti-peyote bill was introduced by Senator Dennis Chávez of New Mexico—the first to reach the floor of the Senate since 1919. In reaction, Collier endeavored to gather a wealth of expert opinion against the bill from several renowned anthropologists (notably Franz Boas and Alfred L. Kroeber), completed by the testimony of Vincenzo Petrullo, Weston La Barre, and Richard Schultes, who had just published their seminal works on the issue. All of these opinions, together with those of other scientists and Native American leaders, were assembled in a document named "Statement against the Chavez Senate Bill 1349" (Boas et al. 1937), which offered a powerful and overwhelming rebuttal of prohibitionists' claims and contributed to the bill quietly disappearing before being examined by the Senate (Maroukis 2012).

From the late 1910s to the years preceding the Second World War, the peyote controversy was thus significantly reconfigured. During this period, Peyotism continued to spread across the United States territory and beyond, well over three hundred miles into Canada (Kahan 2016; Dick and Bradford 2012). The movement succeeded at the same time in securing the support—or, at least, the toleration—of federal authorities; support that will prove enduring, even when drug issues became a central political issue, leading notably to the adoption of the Controlled Substances Act of 1970 (e.g., Olson 1981). Meanwhile, the wave of adoption of anti-peyote state laws remained for a time out of the scope of Peyotists' advocacy efforts, due to their relative inefficiency. The situation however changed after the War. Concerned that state prohibition laws may eventually endanger access to peyote, the NAC endeavored to challenge the constitutionality of these statutes in court and elaborated a new legal strategy in which the involvement of the "second generation" of peyote anthropologists would prove instrumental.

4.2. Cultural Expertise and Strategic Litigation

Between 1957 and 1969, inspired by the success of the civil rights movement, the NAC undertook to challenge anti-peyote legislations in several key states, including New Mexico, Arizona, California, Colorado, and Texas. The strategy developed by the church (Section 4.2.1), based primarily on test cases and occasionally supplemented by legislative lobbying, proved efficient in fighting state prohibition laws (Section 4.2.2). The conflict culminated in the Texas crisis, which threatened to close off access to peyote (Section 4.2.3). In all of these cases, anthropologists acting as expert witnesses—and most notably Omer Stewart—played a crucial role in supporting the legal struggle of the NAC (Section 4.2.4).

4.2.1. Elaborating a Test Case Strategy

It is under the presidency of Frank Takes Gun (1956–1969) that the NAC started to embark on an offensive legal crusade against state anti-peyote laws. Inspired by the success of the National Association for the Advancement of Colored Peoples (NAACP) and the American Civil Liberties Union (ACLU), which culminated in the adoption of the Civil Rights Act in 1964, the NAC considered the opportunity of challenging the constitutionality of these statutes through individual cases, supplementing the strategy with the involvement of anthropologists acting as expert witnesses, a practice that had started to developed since the 1950s (Holden 2011, 2019b; Rodriguez 2018). Take Guns therefore established relationships with the ACLU, and was able to solicit their aid in representing Native American litigants in subsequent cases (Slotkin 1956).

The strategy was first tested in Arizona, where a bitter internal conflict was opposing Navajo on the use of peyote since the early 1940s after the Tribal council had adopted a resolution prohibiting the possession and use of peyote on the reservation (Aberle 1966); two decades of controversy ensued, marking a significant backlash to Commissioner Collier's policy (Dawson 2018; Stewart 1993). Interestingly, the conflict prompted the intervention of anthropologists through national media: in July and November 1951, statements favorable to peyote written by Stewart, La Barre, Slotkin, McAllester, and others, were thus published by Time and Science magazines in reaction to an article particularly hostile to peyote and based on assertions from Dr. Clarence Salisbury, the medical missionary to the Navajo and head of the Navajo Presbyterian Mission (Time 1951a, 1951b; La Barre et al. 1951). A few months after his election, Take Guns consequently took the opportunity of the arrest of Navajo Peyotist Mike Kiyaani to test the legal validity of the Tribal council resolution. A writ of habeas corpus was filed, and, at trial on February 1957, anthropologist James Slotkin was appointed as an expert witness for Kiyaani, supporting the lawyers' argument that the resolution was violating the Free Exercise Clause of the 1st Amendment. Although the case was lost, it convinced the NAC that this legal strategy could prove an efficient weapon against harassment and legal oppression[10].

The first success for the NAC test case strategy occurred in 1960, when the church took the opportunity of the prosecution of Navajo Peyotist Mary Attakai to challenge the constitutionality of the state law prohibiting peyote in Arizona. At trial, anthropologist Omer Stewart testified at length about the peyote religion, alongside psychiatrist Bernard Gorton, who had studied the effects of mescaline at the New York Psychiatric Institute in the early 1950s and maintained that peyote was neither addictive nor harmful. Judge Yale McFate dismissed the charges against Mary Attakai, ruling that the Arizona statute was unconstitutional as applied to the acts of the defendant in the conduct and practice of her religious practice. He notably noted: "The use of peyote is essential to the existence of the peyote religion. Without it, the practice of the religion would be effectively prevented[11]." On 25 April 1961, the Supreme Court of Arizona dismissed the appeal of the decision, marking the first judicial acknowledgement of the consolidation of peyote ceremonial use into a legitimate religious practice.

4.2.2. The Woody Decision (1964) and Subsequent Successes

The most resounding victory in the NAC test case strategy against state anti-peyote laws occurred only a few years later in California. In April 1962, three Navajo railroad workers were arrested after a peyote ceremony was raided in the desert near Needles, California. Jack Woody, Leon B. Anderson, and Dan Dee Nez were charged with illegal possession of peyote in violation of the California anti-peyote law, adopted in 1959 (Stewart 1986). As in the Attakai case, the NAC immediately joined the procedure and arranged for Omer Stewart to provide expert testimony during the trial before the Superior Court in November 1962—alongside Gordon A. Alles, professor of pharmacology at UCLA. The three defendants pleaded not guilty, claiming that their possession of peyote was incident to the observance of their faith and that the state could not constitutionally invoke the statute against them without abridging their right to the free exercise of their religion. The court nonetheless held the defendants guilty and imposed suspended sentences for terms of two to ten years in state prison. Interestingly, Judge Carl B. Hillard expressed reservations with the NAC litigation strategy, noting, "Any plea that might be advanced in behalf of less restrictive treatment of peyote should be addressed to a legislative rather than a judicial remedy." In response to the decision, a bill to accommodate the religious use of peyote was introduced in January 1963 by Nicholas C. Petris, a member of the California State Assembly. Although the bill was defeated in the Senate's Committee on Public Health

---

[10] The peyote prohibition on the Navajo reservation was eventually lifted a decade later. It is now estimated that over half the Tribe's members have adopted peyotism, meaning that about one-fourth of the membership in the NAC is Navajo (Stewart 1993).

[11] Through the intermediary of Omer Stewart, the opinion was published in the American Anthropologist (American Anthropologist 1961).

and Safety, it contributed to the considerable media attention already received by the case at that stage (New York Times 1962; Weeks 1962).

The Superior Court's decision was consequently appealed to the California Second District Court of Appeal in Los Angeles, which upheld the conviction. The case was further appealed to the Supreme Court of California in 1964, which, in an eloquent decision, eventually reversed the judgment against the three Navajo Peyotists. Relying on the Sherbert doctrine recently established by the U.S. Supreme Court, the court asserted that the state failed at demonstrating a compelling interest in the complete prohibition of peyote, founding that the sacramental use of the plant presented only slight danger to the state and to the enforcement of its law, while it constitutes "the sine qua non of defendant's faith" and "incorporates the essence of [their] religious expression." The 21-page decision, delivered on 24 August 1964, and making extensive use of the cultural evidence presented before the Superior Court by Omer Stewart, was written by Justice Matthew Tobriner and concurred in by five of the six other justices. It notably reads,

> [The] right to free religious expression embodies a precious heritage of our history. In a mass society, which presses at every point toward conformity, the protection of a self-expression, however unique, of the individual and the group becomes ever more important. The varying currents of the subcultures that flow into the mainstream of our national life give depth and beauty. We preserve a greater value than an ancient tradition when we protect the rights of the Indians who honestly practiced an old religion in using peyote one night at a meeting in a desert hogan near Needles, California.

Following this resounding legal victory in California, the NAC endeavored to challenge the 1917 anti-peyote law in Colorado, taking the opportunity of the arrest in 1966 of a NAC roadman, Immanuel Trujillo for possession of peyote. Again, Omer Stewart testified at trial, citing the ruling in Woody, and convinced the Colorado court to dismiss the charges against Trujillo and to declare the 1917 law unconstitutional as applied to NAC members.

4.2.3. The Texas Crisis (1967–1969)

The strategy was successfully used one last time, after the state of Texas endeavored to revise its tolerant policy towards peyote by passing the Texas Dangerous Drug Act of 1967, which made the possession of peyote illegal in the state, even for Native Americans. The decision, threatening to cut off the access to peyote, sparked intense and immediate concern throughout the reservations where Peyotism was flourishing. The NAC decided to react forthwith. A few months after the adoption of the statute, Frank Takes Gun directed a young Navajo, David S. Clark, to get deliberately arrested in possession of peyote; the arrest occurred in Laredo in March 1968.

Again, an anthropologist was appointed by the NAC to provide an expert testimony; this time, it was David Aberle, who had just published a monograph on Navajo peyotism (Aberle 1966). The case was handled by Judge E. James Kazen, who relied on the California Supreme Court decision in Woody and found that the Texas indiscriminate prohibition of peyote violated the defendant's right to the free exercise of religion; the charges against Clark were consequently dismissed (Schaefer 2015). The decision was a huge victory for the NAC, but a further effort was needed, as the court's decision had force only in his judicial district. A large delegation of NAC officials, with the help of anthropologist J. Gilbert McAllister from the University of Texas, eventually persuaded in 1969 the Texas legislature to amend its law by exempting members of the NAC from the prohibition (Stewart 1993).

This series of legal victories however tended to produce a judicial understanding of Peyotism attuned to the racial sensibilities of American law, consolidating a reductive narrative of peyote use as exclusively belonging to the indigenous realm (Dawson 2018). Attached to the protection of Native American rights, anthropologists intervening as expert witnesses in these litigations found themselves enrolled in this process of essentialization of Peyotism, and therefore departed from Mooney's wider opposition to the prohibition of peyote.

4.2.4. Anthropologists as Strategic Expert Witnesses

In each one of these legal victories against the state prohibition statutes that symbolized the reconfiguration of the peyote controversy after 1918, anthropologists were directly involved, intervening as crucial expert witnesses in court—and, even if to a lesser extent, by supporting correlated legislative lobbying efforts. Although the precise impact of this mediation role on the final ruling is difficult to assess, the recurrent presence of these scholars undoubtedly constituted a remarkable feature of the NAC strategy. It also arguably reveals how enduring prejudices against Native American rights' claims are, as Peyotists seem to have constantly felt the need to have a "legitimate" intermediary—at least in the eyes of the legal institutions—to give weight to the authenticity of their religious claims (Spivak 1988).

Omer Stewart has, in this respect, been a central element in the NAC strategic litigation approach. As said earlier, he appeared in eight court cases related to the Native American religious right to use peyote in ceremonial settings during that period. He was only replaced at two occasions, when the expertise of anthropologists James Slotkin and David Aberle was deemed more relevant in consideration of the litigants' tribal affiliation and cultural background. To a certain extent, Stewart's involvement in the controversy therefore echoes James Mooney's previous crucial engagement with the legal defense of Peyotism. The modality and the substance of his contribution are however distinguishable from Mooney's in two fundamental ways. Firstly, he substituted the legislative and regulatory mode of intervention of Mooney by a jurisdictional one: expert witnessing. To a large extent, it can be argued that this formal evolution of anthropologists' involvement in the peyote controversy relates both to the development of anthropological expert witnessing since the 1950s (Holden 2019b; Rodriguez 2018), and to the concomitant "juridification" (or "right-based" logic) of the life of the law in the United States (Teubner 1987). Secondly, Stewart—and the "second generation" in general—replaced Mooney's indiscriminate contestation of peyote prohibition by a narrower defense of Native American Peyotists' claim to a limited exemption based on cultural and religious grounds. However, it appears that this reconfiguration of the substance of anthropologists' involvement in the conflicts directly results from a larger movement of essentialization of Peyotism whose rationale has more complex ramifications (Stewart 1993; Dawson 2018). Finally, it should be added here that, contrary to Mooney, Stewart did not experience any form of governmental or academic retaliation as a consequence of his dual position as an expert of Peyotism and an advocate of the movement's religious freedom[12].

Interestingly, Stewart also intervened during this very period in the nascent academic debate over the involvement of anthropologists as expert witnesses in the U.S. He defended an active participation of cultural scholars in litigation processes, and directly opposed arguments identifying practical and ethical issues linked to the specificity of the field. The discussion was initiated by Lawrence Rosen in his seminal article "The Anthropologist as Expert Witness", published in 1977 in American Anthropologist (Rosen 1977), where he notably questioned the adequacy of anthropological knowledge to adversary legal proceedings and the potential distorting influence of such involvement on anthropologists' writings—in anticipation of their potential legal significance. Rosen consequently proposed a set of recommended standards and reforms for anthropological expert witnessing in order to tackle the ethical and deontological issues he identified. Stewart published his response to Rosen's article less than two years after. Against the opinion that anthropologists' involvement in judicial proceedings might lead them to change their opinion or adversely influence their writing, he stated emphatically, "In 25 years as an expert witness I have never experienced any problems of a scholarly or ethical nature" (Stewart 1979)[13].

---

[12] Stewart conserved the chair of the Department of Anthropology at the University of Colorado—which he funded in 1944—until his death in 1991.

[13] Unconvinced by Stewart's arguments, Rosen published his final answer the same year (Rosen 1979). It should be noted here that this debate unfolded in the context of the Mashpee litigation, whose 41-day trial saw the confrontation of anthropologists' and historian's expertise, and was recorded by James Clifford (Clifford 1988).

Another of Stewart's implication in legal proceedings relative to Native American rights provides an interesting supplement to this discussion: Stewart indeed also acted as expert witness for the Indian Land Claims Commission. In this context, he repeatedly cross swords with anthropologist Julian H. Steward (his former professor at the University of Utah), who assisted the U.S. government in a number of cases before the Commission and often denied sufficient social organization to Native American tribes claiming legitimate occupation of contested territories (Stewart 1979; Pinkoski 2008). This frontal opposition of expertise provides an illuminating demonstration of how anthropological knowledge can be employed to advance antagonist political positions in legal proceedings, thereby reviving the enduring debate over cultural expert witnesses' neutrality (Lewis 1988; Mertz 1994).

When he was awarded the Society for Applied Anthropology's Malinowski Award in 1983, Omer Stewart unequivocally noted in his address: "my most important contribution as an applied anthropologist has been to help Indians protect themselves from unjust state laws which outlawed peyote" (Stewart 1983). Native Americans certainly felt the same way; several renowned (and many anonymous) Peyotists indeed wrote vibrant tributes at Stewart's death on December 31, 1991 (Deseret News 1992).

5. Conclusions

This series of victories against the precarious legal barriers that anti-Peyotists had strived to erect against this thriving entheogenic movement did however not put an end to the controversy. The advent of the psychedelic revolution in the 1960s, together with the correlated intensification of the war on drugs indeed threatened the legal protection that Peyotists were able to secure after decades of struggle. Anthropologists continued to intervene in these disputes, although less frequently, as the conflict progressively settled down[14]. It should however be reminded here that the complex evolution of this controversy, which led to the eventual legal protection of Native American Peyotism through a process of essentialization, also resulted in the disqualification—and correlative prohibition—of other forms of peyote use, based on a tacit reenactment of racial categories that continues to pervade the regulation of psychoactive substances (Cavnar and Labate 2016; Dawson 2018).

The two periods considered in this paper constitute remarkable testimonies of the multifaceted and instrumental role that anthropologists have played in this controversy. Notably, the analysis demonstrates that the historical evolution of the conflict, which first played out in legislative arena before migrating to judicial settings, imposed a transformation and a diversification of cultural expertise. Accordingly, these two periods corresponded to two "generations" of peyote anthropologists, which each adopted a predominant mode of legal intervention in support of Peyotists' claims: expert testimonies before legislative bodies for the first generation and expert witnessing before courts for the second. Furthermore, this practical transformation of anthropologists' involvement in the controversy was accompanied by a reconfiguration of their argumentation: with the consolidation of Peyotism into an established religion, anthropologists indeed progressively abandoned the general contestation of the alleged danger of peyote to concentrate their claims on the central and distinctive importance of peyote use for Native Americans, substantiated by a wealth of ethnographic data accumulated during the 20th century. Although ultimately reductive and problematic—notably inasmuch as it fails to integrate the nonrecreational use of peyote by "non-Natives"—it appears that this evolution was made necessary by the way in which Western legal systems conceive indigeneity, and consequently by the nature of the judicial interpretation of cultural argumentation.

For all these reasons, the longstanding legal dispute over the entheogenic use of peyote in the United States holds immense heuristic value for the contemporary reflection on the role and impact of

---

[14] See, for instance, the role of anthropologist Jay C. Fikes in the campaign for the adoption of the 1994 Amendments to the American Indian Religious Freedom Act, which followed the resounding Supreme Court's decision in Smith and allowed for the safeguarding of the exemption scheme and a relative stabilization of the controversy (Maroukis 2012).

cultural expertise in law, and of the various forms that this expertise can take, beyond the conventional focus on anthropological expert witnessing. In this respect, the contribution of James Mooney proved particularly instrumental, notably in regard of its implication in the establishment of the Native American Church, which paved the way for Native American Peyotists' eventual success in protecting their use of peyote. Furthermore, the analysis richly exemplifies the enduring and problematic dual position experienced by anthropologists involved in this type of controversy, navigating between a supposedly impartial position as experts, and an arguably biased engagement as advocates for Native American religious rights. This tension, which had dire professional consequences for Mooney, was arguably even aggravated by the strategic essentialization of Peyotism, leading the "second generation" to substantiate an essentialist narrative of the entheogenic use of peyote that has until now tended to simplify the complexity of the practice.

Funding: This research received no external funding.

Acknowledgments: This research highly beneficiated from the intellectual support provided by the ERC Project "Cultural Expertise in Europe: What is it useful for?—EURO-EXPERT" and the author's participation to the conference Cultural Expertise in Ancient and Modern History convened by EURO-EXPERT on the 4 July 2018 at Oxford.

Conflicts of Interest: The author declares no conflict of interest.

References

Aberle, David F. 1966. *The Peyote Religion among the Navajo*. New York: Wenner Gren Fundation for Anthropological Research.

Aberle, David F., and Omer C. Stewart. 1957. *Navaho and Ute Peyotism: A Chronogical and Distributional Study*. Boulder: University of Colorado Press.

Adams, David W. 1997. *Education for Extinction: American Indians and the Boarding School Experience, 1875–1928*. Lawrence: University of Kansas Press.

Aguirre Beltrán, Gonzalo. 1963. *Medicina y Magia. El Proceso de Aculturación en la Estructura Colonial*. Mexico: Instituto Nacional Indigenista.

American Anthropologist. 1961. Court Decision regarding Peyote and the Native American Church. *American Anthropologist* 63: 1335–37. [CrossRef]

Anderson, Edward F. 1996. *Peyote: The Divine Cactus*. Tucson: University of Arizona Press.

Antell, Judith A., and Malcolm D. Holmes. 2001. The Social Construction of American Indian Drinking: Perceptions of American Indian and White Officials. *Sociological Quarterly* 42: 151–73.

Belcher, Wyatt W. 1953. The Political Leadership of Robert L. Owen. *The Chronicles of Oklahoma* 31: 361–71.

Benciolini, Maria, and Arturo Gutiérrez del Ángel. 2016. From Solid to Frothy: Use of Peyote in the Cora and Huichol Easter in Western Mexico. In *Peyote: History, Tradition, Politics, and Conservation*. Edited by Beatrice C. Labate and Clancy Cavnar. Santa Barbara: Praeger, pp. 171–90.

Boas, Franz. 1938. Truman Michelson. *International Journal of American Linguistics* 9: 113–16. [CrossRef]

Boas, Franz, Alfred L. Kroeber, Aleš Hrdlička, John P. Harrington, Mark R. Harrington, Weston La Barre, Vincenzo M. Petrullo, Richard E. Schultes, Elna Smith, and Chief Lookout. 1937. Statement against the Chavez Senate Bill 1349. *Congressional Record*, February 8.

Bureau of Indian Affairs. 1922. *Peyote: An Abridged Compilation from the Files of the Bureau of Indian Affairs*; Washington: Government Printing Office.

Cavnar, Clancy, and Beatriz C. Labate, eds. 2016. *Prohibition, Religious Freedom, and Human Rights: Regulating Traditional Drug Use*. Berlin: Springer.

Chuchiak, John. 2012. *The Inquisition in New Spain, 1536–1820: A Documentary History*. Baltimore: Johns Hopkins University Press.

Clifford, James. 1988. *The Predicament of Culture: Twentieth-Century Ethnography, Literature, and Art*. Cambridge: Harvard University Press.

Colby, William M. 1978. Routes to Rainy Mountain: A Biography of James Mooney, Ethnologist. Ph.D. dissertation, University of Wisconsin, Madison.

Dawson, Alexander S. 2016. Peyote in the Colonial Imagination. In *Peyote: History, Tradition, Politics, and Conservation*. Edited by Beatrice C. Labate and Clancy Cavnar. Santa Barbara: Praeger, pp. 43–62.

Dawson, Alexander S. 2018. *The Peyote Effect: From the Inquisition to the War on Drugs*. Oakland: University of California Press.

Department of the Interior. 1912. *Annual Report of the Board of Indian Commissioners to the Secretary of the Interior, for Submission to the President*; Washington: Government Printing Office.

Deseret News. 1992. Death: Omer Stewart. *Deseret News*, January 14.

Dick, Erika, and Tolly Bradford. 2012. Peyote on the prairies: Religion, scientists, and Native-newcomer relations in western Canada. *Journal of Canadian Studies* 46: 28–52. [CrossRef]

El-Seedi, Hesham R., Peter A. De Smet, Olof Beck, Göran Possnert, and Jan G. Bruhn. 2005. Prehistoric peyote use: Alkaloid analysis and radiocarbon dating of archaeological specimens of *Lophophora* from Texas. *Journal of Ethnopharmacology* 101: 238–42. [CrossRef]

Foster, George M. 1969. *Applied Anthropology*. Boston: Little, Brown.

Godlaski, Theodore M. 2011. The God within. *Substance Use and Misuse* 46: 1217–22. [CrossRef]

Gormley, Donald C. 1955. The Role of the Expert Witness. *Ethnohistory* 2: 326–46. [CrossRef]

Greenleaf, Richard. 1965. The Inquisition and the Indians of New Spain: A Study in Jurisdictional Confusion. *The Americas* 22: 138–66. [CrossRef]

Grillo, Ralph. 2016. Anthropologists Engaged with the Law (and Lawyers). *Antropologia Pubblica* 2: 3–24.

Hagan, William T. 1993. *Quanah Parker, Comanche Chief*. Norman: University of Oklahoma Press.

Halpern, John H., Andrea R. Sherwood, James I. Hudson, Deborah Yurgelun-Todd, and Harrison G. Pope Jr. 2005. Psychological and Cognitive Effects of Long-Term Peyote Use Among Native Americans. *Biological Psychiatry* 58: 624–31. [CrossRef] [PubMed]

Holden, Livia, ed. 2011. *Cultural Expertise and Litigation: Patterns, Conflicts, Narratives*. New York: Routledge.

Holden, Livia. 2019a. Cultural Expertise and Socio-Legal Studies: Introduction. *Studies in Law, Politics, and Society* 78: 1–12.

Holden, Livia. 2019b. Beyond Anthropological Expert Witnessing: Toward an Integrated Definition of Cultural Expertise. *Studies in Law, Politics, and Society* 78: 181–202.

Irwin, Lee. 1997. Freedom, Law, and Prophecy: A Brief History of Native American Religious Resistance. *American Indian Quarterly* 21: 33–55. [CrossRef]

Jackson, Curtis, and Marcia Galli. 1977. *A History of the Bureau of Indian Affairs and Its Activities among Indians*. San Francisco: R&E Research Associates.

Jahoda, Gloria. 1995. *Trail of Tears: The Story of the American Indian Removal 1813–1855*. New York: Wings Books.

Kahan, Fannie. 2016. *A Culture's Catalyst: Historical Encounters with Peyote and the Native American Church in Canada*. Winnipeg: University of Manitoba Press.

Kroeber, Alfred L. 1902. *The Arapaho*. New York: American Museum of Natural History.

La Barre, Weston. 1938. *The Peyote Cult*. New Haven: Yale University Press.

La Barre, Weston. 1939. Notes on Richard Schultes' "The Appeal of Peyote". *American Anthropologist* 41: 340–42. [CrossRef]

La Barre, Weston, David P. McAllester, James S. Slotkin, Omer C. Stewart, and Sol Tax. 1951. Statement on Peyote. *Science* 114: 582–83. [CrossRef]

León-Portilla, Miguel. 2002. *Bernardino de Sahagún: The First Anthropologist*. Norman: University of Oklahoma Press.

Lewandowski, Tadeusz. 2016. *Red Bird, Red Power: The Life and Legacy of Zitkala-Ša*. Norman: University of Oklahoma Press.

Lewis, Diane. 1973. Anthropology and Colonialism. *Current Anthropology* 14: 581–602. [CrossRef]

Lewis, Ioan M. 1988. Anthropologists for sale? *LSE Quarterly* 2: 49–63.

Lumholtz, Carl. 1902. *Unknown Mexico: A Record of Five Years' Exploration among the Tribes of the Western Sierra Madre*. New York: C. Scribner's Sons.

Mark, Joan. 1982. Francis La Flesche: The American Indian as Anthropologist. *ISIS* 73: 495–510.

Maroukis, Thomas C. 2012. *Peyote Road: Religious Freedom and the Native American Church*. Norman: University of Oklahoma Press.

Martin, Jill E. 2003. "The Greatest Evil" Interpretations Of Indian Prohibition Laws, 1832–1953. *Great Plains Quarterly* 23: 35–53.

Memmi, Albert, and Howard Greenfield. 1967. *The Colonizer and the Colonized*. Boston: Beacon Press.

Mertz, Douglas K. 1994. The Role of the Anthropologist as Expert Witness in Litigation. Paper presented at the Annual Conference of the Alaska Anthropological Association, Anchorage, AK, USA, April 6–9.
Mooney, James. 1891. The Sacred Formulas of the Cherokee. *Bureau of American Ethnology Annual Report* 7: 303–97.
Mooney, James. 1892. A Kiowa Mescal Rattle. *American Anthropologist* 5: 64–65. [CrossRef]
Mooney, James. 1896. The Mescal Plant and Ceremony. *Therapeutic Gazette* 12: 7–11.
Mooney, James. 1897. The Kiowa Peyote Ritual. *Der Urquell* 1: 329–33.
Mooney, James. 2012. *The Ghost-Dance Religion and the Sioux Outbreak of 1890*. Miami: HardPress Publishing.
Morgan, George R., and Omer C. Stewart. 1984. Peyote trade in South Texas. *The Southwestern Historical Quarterly* 87: 270–96.
Moses, L. G. 1978. James Mooney and the Peyote Controversy. *Chronicles of Oklahoma* 56: 127–44.
Moses, L. G. 2002. *The Indian Man: A Biography of James Mooney*. Lincoln: University of Nebraska Press.
Musto, David F. 1999. *The American Disease: Origins of Narcotic Control*. New York: Oxford University Press.
New York Times. 1962. Trial of Navajo Members of the Native American Church. *New York Times*, November 30.
Newsom, Michael deHaven. 2005. Some Kind of Religious Freedom: National Prohibition and the Volstead Act's exemption for the Religious Use of Wine. *Brooklyn Law Review* 70: 739–888.
O'Brien, Sharon L. 1995. Freedom of Religion in Indian Country. *Montana Law Review* 56: 451–84.
Oklahoma, Constitutional Convention. 1907. *Proceedings and Debates of the Constitutional Convention of Oklahoma: Nov. 20, 1906 to March 11, 1907*. Guthrie: Muskogee Printing Co.
Olson, Theodore B. 1981. *Peyote Exemption for Native American Church: Memorandum Opinion For The Chief Counsel, Drug Enforcement Administration*; Washington: Department of Justice.
Petrullo, Vincenzo M. 1934. *The Diabolic Root: A Study of Peyotism, the New Religion Among the Delawares*. Philadelphia: University of Pennsylvania Press.
Philip, Kenneth R. 1977. *John Collier's Crusade for Indian Reform, 1920–1954*. Tucson: University of Arizona Press.
Pinkoski, Marc. 2008. Julian Steward, American anthropology, and colonialism. *Histories of Anthropology Annual* 4: 172–204. [CrossRef]
Prucha, Francis. 1990. *Documents of United States Indian Policy*. Lincoln: University of Nebraska Press.
Quezada, Noemí. 1991. The Inquisition's Repression of Curanderos. In *Cultural Encounters: The Impact of the Inquisition in Spain and the New World*. Edited by Mary Elizabeth Perry and Anne J. Cruz. Berkeley: University of California Press, pp. 37–57.
Rodriguez, Leila. 2018. Introduction: Cultural Expert Testimony in American Legal Proceedings. *Studies in Law, Politics and Society* 74: 1–10.
Rojas-Aréchiga, Mariana, and Joel Flores. 2016. An Overview of Cacti and the Controversial Peyote. In *Peyote: History, Tradition, Politics, and Conservation*. Edited by Beatrice C. Labate and Clancy Cavnar. Santa Barbara: Praeger, pp. 21–42.
Rosemblatt, Karin A. 2018. *The Science and Politics of Race in Mexico and the United States, 1910–1950*. Chapel Hill: University of North Carolina Press.
Rosen, Lawrence. 1977. The Anthropologist as Expert Witness. *American Anthropologist* 79: 555–78. [CrossRef]
Rosen, Lawrence. 1979. Response to Stewart. *American Anthropologist* 81: 111–12. [CrossRef]
Schaefer, Stacy B. 2015. *Amada's Blessings from the Peyote Gardens of South Texas*. Albuquerque: University of New Mexico Press.
Schultes, Richard E. 1938. The Appeal of Peyote (*Lophophora Williamsii*) as a Medicine. *American Anthropologist* 40: 698–715. [CrossRef]
Slotkin, James S. 1951. Early eighteenth century documents on Peyotism north of the Rio Grande. *American Anthropologist* 53: 420–27. [CrossRef]
Slotkin, James S. 1955. Peyotism, 1521–1891. *American Anthropologist* 57: 202–30. [CrossRef]
Slotkin, James S. 1956. *The Peyote Religion: A Study in Indian-white Relations*. Glencoe: Free Press.
Slotkin, James S., and David P. McAllester. 1952. Menomini Peyotism, a Study of Individual Variation in a Primary Group with a Homogeneous Culture. *Transactions of the American Philosophical Society* 42: 565–700. [CrossRef]
Smith, Huston, and Reuben Snake, eds. 1996. *One Nation Under God: The Triumph of the Native American Church*. Santa Fe: Clear Light Publishers.
Spivak, Gayatri C. 1988. Can the subaltern speak? In *Marxism and the Interpretation of Culture*. Edited by Cary Nelson. Basingstoke: Macmillan, pp. 271–313.
Stewart, Omer C. 1941. The Southern Ute peyote cult. *American Anthropologist* 43: 303–8. [CrossRef]

Stewart, Omer C. 1944. Washo-Northern Paiute Peyotism: A Study in Acculturation. *University of California Publications in American Archaeology and Ethnology* 40: 63–141.
Stewart, Omer C. 1948. *Ute Peyotism: A Study of a Cultural Complex*. Boulder: University of Colorado Press.
Stewart, Omer C. 1979. An Expert Witness Answers Rosen. *American Anthropologist* 81: 108–11. [CrossRef]
Stewart, Omer C. 1983. Historical Notes about Applied Anthropology in the United States. *Human Organization* 42: 189–94. [CrossRef]
Stewart, Omer C. 1986. Peyotism in California. *Journal of California and Great Basin Anthropology* 8: 217–25.
Stewart, Omer C. 1993. *Peyote Religion: A History*. Norman: Oklahoma University Press.
Taylor, William. 1996. *Magistrates of the Sacred: Priests and Parishioners in Eighteenth-century Mexico*. Stanford: Stanford University Press.
Terrya, Martin, Karen L. Steelmanb, Tom Guildersonc, Phil Deringd, and Marvin W. Rowee. 2006. Lower Pecos and Coahuila peyote: new radiocarbon dates. *Journal of Archaeological Science* 33: 1017–21. [CrossRef]
Teubner, Gunther, ed. 1987. *Juridification of Social Spheres: A Comparative Analysis in the Areas of Labor, Corporate, Antitrust and Social Welfare Law*. Berlin: Walter de Gruyter.
Time. 1951a. Medicine: Button, Button .... *Time*, June 18, vol. 57.
Time. 1951b. Letters. *Time*, July 9, vol. 28.
U.S. Congress, House, and Committee on Indian Affairs. 1918. *Peyote*; Hearings on H.R. 2614, 67th Cong., 2d sess; Washington: Government Printing Office.
Weeks, Paul. 1962. Indian Use of Peyote to Face Test in Court. *Los Angeles Times*, November 13.
Welsh, Herbert. 1918. *Peyote: An Insidious Evil*. Philadelphia: Indian Rights Association.
Wiedman, Dennis. 2012. Upholding Indigenous Freedoms of Religion and Medicine: Peyotists at the 1906–1908 Oklahoma Constitutional Convention and First Legislature. *American Indian Quarterly* 36: 215–46. [CrossRef] [PubMed]

© 2019 by the author. Licensee MDPI, Basel, Switzerland. This article is an open access article distributed under the terms and conditions of the Creative Commons Attribution (CC BY) license (http://creativecommons.org/licenses/by/4.0/).

Article

Cultural Expertise in Sweden: A History of Its Use

Annika Rabo

Department of Social Anthropology, Stockholm University, 10691 Stockholm, Sweden; annika.rabo@socant.su.se

Received: 25 April 2019; Accepted: 11 September 2019; Published: 17 September 2019

Abstract: This paper is a case study of the use of cultural experts, broadly defined as including mediators and academicians with a variety of backgrounds, in Sweden. It draws on data collected through qualitative interviews with cultural experts, by following court cases through legal documents, mass media and other printed material, and by my own experience as a cultural expert. The paper provides a context to the potential application of the concept of cultural expertise regarding the appointment of such experts by lawyers, prosecutors and courts. It analyzes cases concerning the Sami, the Roma and recent immigrants from Africa and Asia. The Sami cases revolve around conflicts with the Swedish state over rights and ownership. The Roma cases revolve around questions of ethnic discrimination. Cases of immigrants from outside Europe consist of individual criminal cases and asylum. I argue that Swedish ideas—and ideals—of sameness and equality have had an impact on the legal cases that I discuss in this paper. While the legal issues in each of these cases differ, the paper argues that they demonstrate a similarity in how Swedish-majority society manages and even creates cultural differences. I conclude by showing the ways culture, rights, and obligations are understood in courts reflect mainstream trends of Swedish society and suggest the need for cultural expertise in the form of interdisciplinary collaboration.

Keywords: experts; cultural experts; court cases; Sweden; Sami; Roma; immigrants

---

1. Introduction

"In just a short while the ethnic composition of the Swedish population has changed in a noticeable way without greater conflicts between different groups. Lately, however an increased social segregation with ethnic components, has been observed" (SOU 1996, p. 55).[1]

These are the opening sentences of the summary of a 500-page official government report *Sweden, entitled The Future and Multiculturalism*,[2] by the parliamentary Immigrant Committee which worked between April 1995 and April 1996. It consisted of 12 members of parliament and was chaired by the governor of a northern province. Experts, or *sakkunniga*,[3] from various ministries were used, and a number of people with expertise in migration and integration issues were consulted. The report underlines that Sweden has become a multicultural society with around 300,000 born in another Nordic country, 300,000 born in other European countries, and 320,000 born in the rest of the world. In addition, 700,000 persons are born in Sweden but with one or both parents born outside the country.[4]

The opening paragraphs in the report are significant, not by stressing that Sweden has changed though the presence of many immigrants, but that Sweden's multiculturalism is caused by this new ethnic composition of the country. Researchers point out that Sweden has had a long history of

---

[1] All translations from Swedish to English are my own. Original texts in English will be indicated.
[2] The Swedish word is actually *mångfald*—more akin to *diversity*—but it is commonly translated as multiculturalism.
[3] *Sakkunnig* (i.e., "those who know their thing") has a slightly different semantic field compared to *expert*. It was interesting that the Committee had used both *sakkunniga* and *experter* in their work. For sake of simplicity I will use the term *expert*.
[4] Since the mid-1990 these numbers have changed. In late 2017, according to official statistics, almost 19% of the population was born outside Sweden.

immigration, and that the country has always been linguistically, culturally and ethnically diverse (e.g., Svanberg and Tydén 2005). Yet, the idea of a homogenous Sweden still persists. There is a tension in how the state and public agencies have viewed—and still view—sameness and difference among the population. *Diversity* and *multiculturalism* are lauded but are simultaneously perceived as divisive and even dangerous. It was only in 2000, for example, that Sweden ratified the Council of Europe's *Convention for Protection of National Minorities*, and the *European Convention on Minority Languages*. Jews, Roma, Tornedalers, Sweden-Finns and Sami were then recognized as national minorities. The Sami were also given the status as indigenous people. Jiddish, Romani Chib, Finnish, Meänkieli, and the different Sami languages and dialects were simultaneously recognized as national minority languages[5]. These national minorities have very different historical relations to Sweden and to the Swedish state, and very different relations to experts who have either helped, or blocked, their demands for recognition. In turn, these relations are different from the ones formed by the more recent non-Nordic immigrants, who today vastly outnumber the national minorities.[6]

In this article I will look at the history and use of cultural experts—persons who "locate and describe relevant facts in light of the particular background of the claimants, litigant or the accused person(s), and in some cases the victim(s)" (Holden 2011, p. 2; Holden 2019b, pp. 199–200) in Swedish cases involving national minorities and newly arrived immigrants. The court is an excellent arena to analyze how cultural differences and similarities are implicitly understood, promoted or managed. The material is based on face-to-face and e-mail interviews with academic colleagues in anthropology, law, political science, social work, theology and religious studies. I have also followed the paper trail of some legal cases. However, given the novelty of the theoretical underpinning of cultural expertise, instead of engaging in an in-depth but necessarily selective analysis, I have decided to provide a general overview of the use of cultural expertise in Sweden in a narrative format that sometimes interweaves with verbatim extracts of my interviews.

2. Experts in and out of Court

In Swedish courts, the so-called free sifting/consideration of evidence (*fri bevisprövning*) is used. Unlike in Anglo-Saxon legal tradition, there are, in principle, no limitations concerning the sources that can be used by the parties in a trial. The court decides the value of each piece of evidence and assesses the sum of information given. The principle of free sifting of evidence, according to the legal scholars that I interviewed, opens up for the possibility of using all kinds of nonlegal experts in court. However, they noted that the conceptualization of "cultural experts" is new to them.[7] Claes Lernestedt, who is a professor of penal law, said that in cases of criminal law involving physical injury, or psychological illness or deficiencies, experts are routinely acting as witnesses, or sending in statements, but in criminal cases involving sex, for example, the court sees itself fit to have expertise. However, at least three types of Swedish litigation include some kind of cultural expertise: those involving the Sami, Roma, and immigrants.

Historically, academicians have played a very important role in policy making and in public debates in Sweden. In the 19th century particularly, medical doctors came to supplant the expertise of the Swedish clergy as arbiters of human behavior in the name of progress and modernity, both inside and outside the court. Policies to modernize and develop Sweden and its inhabitants were prevalent from the 1930s to the 1960s, and experts of different kinds were used to push for, and legitimize, social reforms. In this social engineering endeavor, citizens deemed underdeveloped were powerless to protest. In the past, different kinds of experts have been very important in supporting the claims of the state, and public authorities, against the interests of the Sami and the Roma. In the

---

[5] For government policy, see (Government Offices of Sweden 2007)
[6] Statistics and registers based on ethnicity or religion is not allowed in Sweden. In official statistics, only country of birth is noted (SCB 2018).
[7] Cultural expert (*kulturexpert*) is not an officially used concept in Sweden.

contemporary period, cultural experts acting as expert witnesses in Swedish cases of litigation come from social activism, public relations, academia, or other institutional appointments on behalf of either side in conflict.

In the following section, I give a brief overview of the historical trajectory of the Sami and the Roma in Sweden, as well as the history of recent immigration to Sweden. This is followed by cases of litigations in which Sami and Roma people have been involved. Then the emergence of experts in the culture of non-European immigrants is discussed, followed by expert involvement in some cases of violent crimes which have received public attention. Subsequently, the relations between law, experts and culture are discussed, and I conclude by analyzing how experts are part of both rejecting and affirming cultural differences in contemporary Sweden.

3. The Sami, the Roma, and the New Immigrants

The Sami had been present in the northern part of Fenno-Scandia long before the establishment of states in the region. In the 14th century, the boundaries of a Swedish state expanded northwards, and the Sami were associated with long-distance trade in meat, fish, and furs—goods which were coveted in the south. The relations between the crown and the Sami were for centuries generally peaceful, and their rights over land were recognized. From the middle of the 17th century until the beginning of the 20th century, Sami villages in the far north of Sweden were divided into so-called taxed-land. Initially, such land was treated as inalienable property on which the villagers paid tax. Towards the end of the 17th century, regional representatives of the state started to claim that the land belonged to the crown. During the 19th century, when the natural resources in the north—forests, water, and iron ore—became essential for Swedish industrial development, the rights of the Sami diminished (see Lundmark 2006). In the late 19th century, a law was passed which regulated the rights of Sami reindeer herders. As a consequence, this particular activity became the basis of how, and for what purposes, the state recognized the Sami. The Swedish authorities have made a sharp distinction—in fact, created a legal difference—between reindeer-herding Sami and Sami with no reindeers. This legal difference has also been the cause of intra-Sami conflicts.[8] In the following section, the Sami cases of litigation concern the Sami organized in reindeer villages.

The first Roma probably reached Sweden in the 16th century (Nafstad 2016). Other groups of Roma came from France and Russia in the end of the 19th century. A large subgroup arrived from Finland in the 1950s, and in the 1960s, Roma from parts of Europe arrived. After the turn of the 21st century, finally, Roma from the Balkans, Bulgaria, and Rumania also arrived. In 2014, the government issued a white paper, documenting how, in the first half of the 21st century, the Roma had been denied the right to settle, how Roma children had been taken from their parents, and how Roma women had been sterilized, all underlining that they were not seen as part of society but as inferior outsiders (Ds 2014, p. 8). This paper focuses on cases of litigation where the Roma accuse individuals or the state of ethnic discrimination.

After World War II, Sweden became a country of immigration rather than of emigration.[9] The Swedish industries were in great need of workers and most came from neighboring countries, as noted above, and particularly from Finland. In the late 1950s and the 1960s, many also came from Italy, Greece, the former Yugoslavia, and Turkey. In the late 1970s, labor migration more or less came to an end, and instead immigrants have been people seeking refuge in the country and persons seeking family reunification. For decades, persons born in Finland constituted the most numerous group born outside Sweden. Now persons born in Syria have taken that place, followed by those born in Finland, Iraq, and Iran.[10] This means that a great many of the immigrants who have arrived in the last few

---

[8] For analysis of this complicated history, see Mörkenstam (2002).
[9] About 25% of the population left Sweden, mainly for the USA, from the early 19th to the early 20th century.
[10] Finns have lost 'the lead' because they are an ageing group with limited 'replenishment' from Finland.

decades come from countries with a Muslim majority population. In the eyes of certain segments of the population, the emblematic immigrant is a Muslim and associated with a particular culture which may lead to gender-based crimes reflecting patriarchal values. The discussion in this paper touches on the role of experts in asylum cases but mainly focuses on cases where immigrants have been accused of violent crimes.

4. Sami Court Cases

The Sami, as much as the Roma, have for a long time been subjected to, and oppressed by, religious, medical, educational, and legal experts at the service of the Swedish state and official policies.[11] But they have also organized themselves and found their own experts, from within or outside their own associations. In the Sami case, the legal battles have focused on rights to land and control over hunting and fishing. The most famous case was the 'Taxed mountain case' (*Skattefjällsmålet*), in which Sami villages sued the Swedish state to gain better and more secure access to land and water. The case started in 1966 and continued until 1981, passing through all instances. No other legal case in Sweden has continued for so long and no other verdict, which covered 100 pages, has been so extensive. Experts on law and history were used by both sides. The state used its experts to claim the historical right of the crown in the north of Sweden. The Sami used historians with expertise on the development of their settlements in the north. In the end, the Sami villages lost against the Swedish state and had to pay for the lengthy process. But the verdict also stated that nomadic people can acquire ownership rights to land and water by having used it since 'time immemorial' (*urminnes hävd*) or by occupying 'empty land'.[12]

In 1990, private landowners and a forestry company in the region close to that of the Taxed mountain case province sued five Sami villages claiming that they had no customary rights (*sedvanerätt*) to graze their herds in nonmountain areas. This time, it was not the state, but private interests against the Sami. Six years later, a district court pronounced that the Sami had lost the case. The Sami took it to a court of appeal but lost in 2002, and in 2004, the supreme court decided not to take on the case.[13] This loss made land-owners further north take other Sami villages to court. But this time, another district court judged that the Sami had the right to herd reindeers on the land. The court of appeal gave the same verdict, as did the supreme court in 2011. This case was the first won by the Sami after 40 years of legal battles. There have been other legal cases which have resulted in a distinction between *rights based on time immemorial*, and *customary rights*. The first concerns the right based on usage for such a long time, in that no one can remember when it started. The second is based on the use having been accepted for a long time, thus making it normal. Legal perception has shifted so that customary use is enough for the Sami to have the right to graze private lands. This has been an advantage for the Sami who are seldom able to produce documents concerning use since time immemorial.

Another bone of contention has been the right to hunt and fish in the mountain areas in the north of Sweden, which the state regards as owned by the crown. In 1992, the Swedish parliament decided to liberalize access to hunting and fishing in these areas. The Sami protested in various ways. In 2009, the National Sami Organization and the Sami village of Girjas sued the state in a district court in the far north, claiming that their rights had been undermined through the new law. The case took a long time to be heard, and when it did in 2015, the Sami and more than 50 researchers from a great many disciplines in the humanities and social sciences were outraged by the vocabulary used by the experts and witnesses of the state. The researchers made a petition claiming that the use of research about the Sami on the part of the Swedish state was flawed. "Years of Swedish and international research is rejected and the language used is a remnant from the era of race biology" (*Dagens Nyheter* 2015).

---

[11] For Ph.D. dissertations on the problematic and often offensive relation between the state and the Roma, see e.g., Runcis (1998), Olgaç Rodell (2006), Nafstad (2016), the state and the Sami, e.g., Beach (1981), Mörkenstam (1999).
[12] For texts in English concerning this case, see Jahreskog (1982).
[13] The cases were very expensive for the villages, and they ended up with a debt of about 1.7 million euros.

In February 201,6 the district court decided in favor of the Sami village. The Swedish state appealed. In 2018 the court of appeal, however, decided that while Girjas village holds rights to fishing and hunting, these rights are shared with the state. The case reached the supreme court, and the session is scheduled to take place between 2 September and 10 October 2019.

In the Taxed mountain case, both the Swedish state and the Sami, as noted above, used experts on history and the legal history of the north. The Sami have also increasingly developed their own expertise and been able to find lawyers who can represent them. All these kinds of experts fall into the integrated definition of cultural expertise (Holden 2019a).

5. Roma Court Cases

In November 2013, the largest Swedish daily, *Dagens Nyheter*, published news that the police in the southern city of Malmö had a register containing the names of 4700 Roma, or people closely linked to Roma individuals. One thousand were children and 200 were deceased. The police claimed that the register fulfilled the purpose of criminal investigations, but the public authority for security and integrity quickly decided that the register was against the law. However, when asked, the judiciary did not identify the register as an ethnic directory. The Chancellor of Justice instead decided that the personal integrity of all individuals on the register had been violated and awarded everyone whose name was on it 5000 Swedish kronor.[14] Many Roma were dismayed that the state did not recognize that they had been registered because of their ethnic background, and some wanted to appeal. In March 2015, 11 of those registered—three of them children—sued the state, with the help of the Civil Rights Defenders.[15] The case was heard in the district court of Stockholm, and a year and a half later, the Roma won the case against the state. The court decided that they had been registered *only* because of their ethnic background, and each litigant was awarded 30,000 Swedish kronor. The state brought the case to the court of appeal but lost and instead settled the verdict of the district court. The state could not show that the register was unrelated to ethnic discrimination. A month later, at the end of May 2017, the Chancellor of Justice, in a surprising move, decided that all persons in the police register would be entitled to the same amount as that awarded to the 11 persons in the court case. They would have to apply individually for the compensation, and if all did, this would amount to the largest damages paid by the Swedish state, caused by a single event. The damages—164 million kronor—would be paid by the police authority.

This court case is unusual, not only because it was won by the Roma, but also because it involved so many people. The most reported cases of discrimination in Sweden concern individual Roma or Roma families who are prevented from entering shops, hotels, restaurants or denied renting an apartment. In the summer of 1980, for example, the owner of a camping site in the middle of Sweden put up a sign saying that Roma were not welcome. A family was denied entry but filed a complaint, and the district attorney sued the owners. The district court judged that this was a case of agitation against an ethnic group (*hets mot folkgrupp*) and that the owner must pay a fine. In the court of appeal, the owner also received a conditional sentence. In the supreme court, finally, the owner was judged to have agitated against an ethnic group, but the conditional sentence was removed.

In another example, from 1996, the district attorney in a southern town prosecuted the owners of a retail outlet. They denied access to Roma women because they claimed that their voluminous skirts were used to hide stolen goods. One Roma woman went to the outlet together with a journalist. She was not allowed to enter, a fracas erupted, the case got media attention, and the woman filed a complaint. The owners claimed that they denied access to *all* with large skirts. The district court could not find that she had been discriminated against because of her ethnic background, but the attorney

---

[14] Ten kronor is about one euro.
[15] Civil Rights Defenders (previously known as the Swedish Helsinki Committee for Human Rights) is an independent expert organization founded in Stockholm in 1982 with the aim of defending human rights, in particular people's civil and political rights.

continued to the court of appeal. This court concluded in favor of the Roma woman, but the owners of the outlet took the case to the Supreme Court. In September 1999, the verdict of the court of appeal was decided, and the owners had to pay a fine to the state and 5000 kronor in damages to the woman.

In the cases above, experts were not instructed systematically. Yet the Roma have become organized in new ways and have spokespersons of different kinds. In the case of the Roma women and their skirts, Karl-Olov Arnstberg, an ethnologist with research experience on the Roma, was appointed to testify on the clothing patterns of different groups in Sweden. He underlined that among the Roma with a Finnish background, the large and heavy skirt was, more or less, mandatory for adult women. This kind of skirt, in the eyes of the public at large, typically signals that the bearer is Roma. The outlet owners could, hence, not claim that they were simply preventing women in general that wear large skirts. In the large register case, there was an expert witness in the district court who testified on the long history of Roma ethnic registers—the Nazis being the most notorious for keeping such records. Such a history has affected the well-being of the Roma in a very negative way. Fred Taikon, a Roma activist and editor of the journal *É Romani Glinda*, was among the ones who sued the Swedish state. Being on the huge police register has negatively affected many of the Roma, he told me. "It is still with us. My grandchild cannot speak about it. He gets psychological problems if he has to contact the police for any reason due also to previous instances of discrimination ... For the register trial we had no access to psychological counselling, which we really needed. And there are other cases ... The social services have forcibly taken so many of our children and this has been traumatic for both parents and children ... "

The Roma have been particularly vulnerable to ill treatment and outright discrimination, by a segment of the authorities who were backed by their experts. The Equality Ombudsman, DO,[16] gets frequent reports from the Roma about discrimination. "Last year we had about fifty ... which is about average for a long time. But this is probably only the tip of an iceberg", according to Lars Lindgren who works as an investigator at DO (*Dagens Nyheter* 2014). Ingrid Schiöler, who has fought for the rights of the Roma for the past 40 years, told me that she has worked on cases involving young Roma and the social services, produced expert reports supporting Roma asylum seekers, and represented Roma in litigations involving the social services: "I have tried to underline that we have a legal framework for the rights of minorities and that the Roma are, in fact a national minority. The typical response from the official representatives of the majority of society has been to claim that 'here we treat all people in the same manner and we make no exceptions.'" In addition to showing an uneven but de facto well-known use of cultural experts and cultural expertise, Roma litigation points at a major component of justice's perception in Sweden: the primacy of formal equality before the law; or in other words, the idea that taking into consideration the context of facts and litigants may amount to an undue impact on the very notion of justice.

6. Experts on 'New Immigrants'

Who are the experts used in court cases and litigation involving non-European immigrants and refugees? To find out more, I corresponded with a number of scholars specialized in research on Islam and Muslims. One was Jan Hjärpe, the best-known scholar of Islam in Sweden, and the first to be appointed as a professor of contemporary Islam in Sweden in 1983. Jan Hjärpe has published extensively also for a general audience and has given frequent popular lectures, as well as making media appearances. He wrote that in the almost 50 years in which he has been active in academia, he has only been appointed as an expert in three trials. However, like many other scholars of Islam and Muslims, he has frequently been asked by lawyers to write statements to give a broad context of

---

[16] The Equality Ombudsman (DO) is a government agency that works on behalf of the Swedish parliament and government to promote equal rights and opportunities and to combat discrimination. In Swedish, the agency is actually called 'the discrimination ombudsman.'

the situation of their clients. "In general it has been cases of deportation where I have been asked to assess the risk for persons to be deported. The questions have been put by the legal representatives of the person to be deported. In general, they ask questions about legal issues related to Islamic jurisprudence and to legal practice in different areas but also questions about jurisdiction; the state or the family. I have also written statements on questions of apostasy, family law, and custody of children. The initiative to find me and ask me for my opinion has typically come from a (private) person who had become engaged in the case. All in all I must have written between 50 and 100 statements throughout the years, mostly in the 1980s, more seldom nowadays.[17] These statements were written and presented in court without me being present." This kind of cultural expertise is similar to the practice of expert report writing described by sociolegal scholarship in the United Kingdom (Good 2006; Holden 2011), where the expert's duty is to the court. However, more often than not, it has been rather perceived in terms of cultural defense in which the expert takes sides and uses cultural expertise for the defense (Renteln 2004).

He continued to tell me that he had been called as an expert witness a few times where the case was later not brought to trial because the parties involved had solved the issue themselves, with the help of the extended families. In fact, the plaint from which the case originated was apparently a strategy to exert pressure on one of the parties in the internal negotiations. One of his appointments as an expert in court concerned a trial involving the adoption of Syrians. The case was very muddled, he recounted, and ultimately involved the question of the religious leadership among a branch of the Alawis in Syria. Hjärpe was convinced that the case must have been a very strange experience for the judge and the lay judges. Another case, details about which he hardly remembered anymore, concerned violence between two families with immigrant backgrounds. And then, there was a notorious case in 1989 concerning hate speech against Jews on a radio channel (Radio Islam) which an immigrant from North Africa had started. Hjärpe, and another religious studies scholar, were called in as experts by the defense. The case was widely covered in mass media before, during and after the trial, and the two scholars were generally—and wrongly—portrayed as defending the views of the accused. The accused was sentenced to six months in prison.[18]

Other scholars of Islam and Muslims have told me that although they have written many statements for various court cases, they have seldom been called as experts to trials. Professor Jonas Otterbeck said he had been called twice; one case of threat and the other of religious discrimination. "In the latter case I made a written statement, as well as answered questions in court." Mohammad Fazlhashemi, the first Swedish professor in Islamic theology, and a scholar with particular expertise on Shi'a theology and jurisprudence, has been contacted by a few lawyers working for women born in Afghanistan. They were seeking divorce in Sweden through the Shi'a *talaq ghi'abi*, which can be applied when the husband has disappeared or refuses to be contacted. "These are the only family law cases I have been involved in. But I have written on the opinions in Islamic jurisprudence—both Sunni and Shi'a views—on desecration of corpses. It was in a case on war crimes in the south of Sweden, which passed through both the district court and the court of appeal. I was asked by the prosecutor, who wanted to know if there is support for desecration of corpses in Islamic jurisprudence. The accused had apparently tried to hide behind religion to explain his hideous act. On another occasion I have written a statement on various interpretations concerning the shaking of hands between women and men in Islamic jurisprudence. It was DO (the Ombudsman for Equality) who asked me. Later on I was also called to answer questions during the session at the Labor Court." In Swedish mass media, there have been much debated cases of Muslim men refusing to shake hands with women. In a few cases, their employer tried to fire them. The Ombudsman for Equality was called in and the scholar was

---

[17] In large part thanks to Jan Hjärpe, the study of contemporary Islam and Muslims has expanded considerably in Sweden, and hence, the pool of potential experts has increased since the 1990s.
[18] In the logic of much contemporary racism, the convicted man has since become strongly aligned with extreme right-wing Nordic supremacist groups.

instructed as the expert at the Labor Court.[19] In 2019, Mohammad Fazlhashemi was appointed by the prosecutor as an expert in a case where a man had posed with dead bodies and posted pictures on social media. This person had taken part in battles against the Islamic State. He was sentenced for war crimes by the court and sent to prison.

This very rapid survey of cultural expertise for litigation and legal proceedings involving so-called new immigrants confirms my previous observation regarding, on the one hand, the difficulty to conceptualize cultural expertise and identify cultural experts in Sweden, and on the other, the increasing but uneven occurrence of the appointment of experts that according to Holden's definition would be qualified as cultural experts.

7. Violent Crimes

Reading or hearing about the details in the cases of assault, torture or killing of young children is, of course, very distressing. Jan Hjärpe later wrote: "I remember that I forgot to mention a case where the prosecutor if I remember rightly called me. It was the case in the town of Karlskrona where a young girl was beaten to death by her caretakers. I was really of little use in that case, unlike the psychological expertise but I was very impressed by the speed and competence of the simultaneous interpreters."[20]

This case was extensively covered in Swedish mass media in 2014 and 2015 and concerned the death, by brutal beating, of an eight-year-old girl who had arrived from the Gaza Strip a year earlier to live with a maternal uncle and his wife and their two children—a new-born and a child of three. According to newspaper reports, the girl had been sent from Gaza by her parents to overcome trauma from the war. She had quite quickly adjusted to her Swedish school. But there were a number of reports from the social services that her caretakers were not treating her well. They, however, did not intervene, and a year after she had arrived in Sweden, she was dead. The case against the caretakers was never framed in terms of 'religion' or 'culture', and the psychiatric assessment declared them both sane. The uncle was sentenced to life imprisonment and so was the aunt. The district court had given the man a lower sentence, since most of the battering had been committed by the woman, but the court of appeal increased his sentence, claiming he was equally culpable. This case had tragic repercussions. Public and bureaucratic blame for the lack of action was put at the door of the school's head teacher. Although he apparently had done nothing wrong, he was sacked and accused of neglect. He became depressed and later tried to commit suicide. His name and reputation were later rehabilitated.

Another twist to this case was that the Swedish Board of Migration in 2017 granted residence permits in Sweden—due to the distressing circumstances—to the parents of the dead girl and to her three siblings. The mother was not happy with this legal status and appealed to obtain refugee status for herself and her children, in order to ensure that they would never be sent back to Gaza. She was afraid that her husband's relatives regarded her as guilty of the murder of her daughter, since she had placed her with her own relatives in Sweden. According to a news report, she said that if she was forced to return, "they would pressure my husband to divorce me and then they would take the children. The family rules more than the individual, and they think they have to avenge the girl." (*Svt Nyheter* 2017).

8. Culture, Law and Experts

It was law professor Claes Lernestedt who alerted me to one of the few cases where an anthropologist had been used as an expert in a criminal case. "There is a case which I frequently use when I teach, where an anthropologist was called in to explain Congolese spirit possession . . . "

---

[19] In another case in April 2018, the Labor Court decided it was discriminatory to fire a female substitute teacher from a (semiprivate) school because she would not shake hands with male colleagues.

[20] For a comparative discussion on translators as experts, see Bouillier (2011).

This case came to trial in a district court in 2000 when three adults—two women and a man—were accused of having killed one child and severely injuring another, both in their care. The accused adults explained that the children had been bewitched (or were witches). The judgement from the district court is more than 40 pages long. It includes a rather detailed description of what happened to the two children during the three days of Christmas, when they were subjected to torture. The three adults had a fairly uniform description of the events, and all three claimed that they had tried to exorcise witchcraft. The statement of the anthropologist, Kajsa Ekholm Friedman, with fieldwork experience from Congo-Kinshasa, is summarized in less than a page. According to the text, she stated that "there are clear differences between the way a Congolese and a Swede understand reality. In Congo evil spirits and witches are part of reality. Personal problems and misfortune are often explained by evil spirits and witches." She also explained that all through the 20th century, there have been movements to cleanse villages from witches. These movements have been more or less violent, and sometimes those accused of being witches have died. "In Congo it is most common that older relatives are perceived to be witches. It is unusual that children are accused, but during the 1990s this had become more frequent in the Kinshasa area." In the assessment of the crime, the court returns to the question of motive and states that this is totally strange "in our culture", but—according to the anthropologist—very real for a great many in Congo-Kinshasa. The court finds "no reason to distrust the accused when they claim that the children were possessed by evil spirits, that they were witches." But when it comes to judging their actions "—in the first case if this constitutes a crime—this must be done according to the Swedish legal system." The man was sentenced to life imprisonment, the two women were sentenced to four years in prison each, and one was sentenced to deportation without the right to return. Two months later the court of appeal affirmed these judgements. The court thus chose, according to Lernestedt, to ignore the beliefs of the accused. In this case, the 'cultural expert' gave a context to the events, but this context was not taken into account by the court. He calls this a legal silence and comments: "What I find provoking in this case is not necessarily the final outcome but the road to it." (Lernestedt 2014, p. 17).[21]

Apart from this case, there have been, as far as I know, three others involving children being seen as witches or possessed by evil spirits tried in Swedish courts in the 21st century. In one case, a man was sentenced to one year in prison in 2003 for having assaulted and battered three young girls during three years, and also for having taken them to Congo for exorcism. The two other cases were both tried in a district court in southwest Sweden in 2013. These cases also involved immigrants from Congo accused of aggravated assault on preteenage girls. In one of them, two caretakers and two priests were accused and acquitted by the district court but sentenced—except for one of the priests—by the court of appeal.

Josef Nsumbu, a doctor of theology and pastor in *Missionskyrkan* in the town of Borås, was called as an expert. He explained that in Congo, there are perceptions that children may become possessed by evil spirits and that these spirits can be exorcised in different ways. Such ideas combine old traditions and Christianity, he explained. The district court claimed that the evidence for assault was weak and that exorcism is common in many Christian churches. The court of appeal, however, underlined that although the accused had strong religious motivations, belief cannot legitimate that children are treated in such a way. The priest was sentenced to one year and three months in prison, the man acting as a father to the children was sentenced to two and a half years, and the acting mother to two years.

The last case involved assault committed between 2007 and 2008 but tried in 2013. Here the caretakers were sentenced by the district court. It seems the court had 'learned a lesson' from its previous case a few months earlier, because they sentenced the acting father to one year in prison and the acting mother to eight months. The court declared that the couple had lived in the belief that the

---

[21] English in the original.

girl was a witch. "It is not punishable to believe in witches, and the case is not about what is the right or wrong belief." The court claimed that "there is no god who thinks that children are evil."

Cases of so-called female genital mutilation (FGM) are, like witchcraft, in Sweden mainly associated with immigrants from the African continent. In 1982, Sweden was the first country in the West to pass a law against female genital mutilation. But it was not until the 1990s—with the arrival of many Somali refugees—that the issue came to the fore and became extensively discussed in public (Johnsdotter 2008a, p. 161). Sara Johnsdotter, professor of medical anthropology, has both followed and written extensively about these debates and the legal cases of FGM in Sweden and elsewhere (Johnsdotter 2008b; Mestre i Mestre and Johnsdotter 2019). She was an expert witness in the first ever FGM trial in Sweden. A father, habitually residing in Sweden, was accused of participating in the circumcision/mutilation of his 12-year-old daughter when in Somalia. He was sentenced to two years in prison in a district court. The sentence was reaffirmed by a court of appeal. Johnsdotter argued that the case against the father was deeply flawed, not least because men never take part in FGM. She was also an expert witness in a Danish case where both parents were sentenced although it was not proved that their daughters had, in fact, been circumcised. "In both these cases, I think that the cultural expert did not play any major role. The (political) wish to sentence was too strong, just as the idea of the prevalence of this phenomenon among immigrant communities," Johnsdotter wrote to me in an email.

Johnsdotter's engagement and field of expertise outside asylum cases is rare. Most fellow anthropologists I asked about being experts in cases of litigation told me that they—like religious studies scholars—had not been approached by lawyers except in asylum cases. Sverker Finnström, with expertise on Uganda, has written statements for cases in Sweden, the UK, and the USA. Additionally, I have been contacted by lawyers representing asylum seekers threatened with expulsion. Especially, I have been asked to vouch for the great probability that the expelled would become the victim of family feuding, or 'honor violence', if they were forced to return. In May 2018, for example, I was contacted by a Swedish lawyer looking for information in support of an asylum claim for a Palestinian man. She found that more than a decade earlier, I had been asked by a lawyer in Australia about honor crimes in Jordan. The Swedish lawyer sent me an excerpt from the report by the Australian lawyer, quoting me. I had agreed that in Jordan, men who are accused of having illicit affairs can be subject to threats, adding that to my knowledge, no protection was available from the Jordanian state. However, I also wrote that I had never come across a case in which a man had been killed in an honor crime, since women are generally blamed when a case involves illicit sex. The Swedish lawyer then wanted me to make a statement about the risks for her Palestinian client. He had been accused and tried for sexual harassment (in Jordan) of "a woman from a powerful clan whose husband works in the Royal Guard who might suspect that there was a mutual sexual relation between his wife and the Palestinian man." I was very reluctant to claim anything in this case and was relieved that I could guide her to two young colleagues with up-to-date fieldwork experience in Jordan and Palestine.

9. Conclusions: The Management of Similarities and Differences

The cases discussed in this article call for deeper analysis from the perspective of cultural expertise as an umbrella concept that spans across a variety of legal fields and calls for different kinds of experts. How can differences and similarities be discerned in the cases discussed above? And what roles—if any—have the experts played to downplay, produce or manage differences and similarities? The categories chosen—Sami, Roma, and new immigrants—are, as stated, very different. Cases discussed involving Sami demonstrate that the conflicts between them and the state, or private landholders or companies, are, in the contemporary period, seldom framed in terms of 'culture', but rather minority rights.[22] The Roma, as shown, still have to struggle against implicit perceptions on the part of the authorities and society at large that they have a deviant 'culture' which can be

---

[22] For interesting discussion on a 'rights discourse' versus a 'culture discourse' see (Good 2008).

linked to particular nondesired behavior. Experts supporting Roma have to argue that to have equal access to justice demands an acknowledgement of difference. The cases discussed involving 'new immigrants' span a wider legal field and cover both civil and criminal law. The case of the bewitched children where the court declared that no god thinks children are evil is interesting. The beliefs of the accused were not doubted, but their 'rationality' was, since all gods are good to children. Apart from the blatantly false statement regarding the fact that gods would be necessarily good towards children, there is an unquestioned assumption that in Sweden, god is kind and benevolent, and hence, also the state is good and benevolent. If we accept cultural expertise in the broad definition proposed by Holden, the question that begs for an answer in the Swedish context is if, and how, the special knowledge brought in court by cultural expertise legitimizes special rights.

In cases of migration and asylum law, a discourse of culture is often tapped into, on the part of clients and their lawyers, even if that concept is not used explicitly. The lawyer who wanted me to argue in favor of her client to avoid expulsion, certainly did. Among mainstream Swedes, the Middle East, and the Muslim world more broadly, is closely associated with patriarchy, tribalism, a lack of gender equality, and with so-called honor crimes. A defense, or an appeal for the right to remain in Sweden, is thus not uncommonly framed as a way to escape from such phenomena. The mother from Gaza also used these perceptions when she wanted a more secure refugee status rather than simply a residence permit, by framing a potential threat from her in-laws in terms of family honor.

In popular and populist discourse—in contrast to debates among legal specialists—honor crimes, and female genital mutilation, for example, are seen as a typical, yet repulsive, part of 'immigrant culture'. One of my informants, Daniel Hedlund, a legal scholar specialized in children and migration law, noted that the concept of 'cultural competence' was, for a while in the 1990s, popular among Swedish bureaucracies and administrative bodies. "After that it was exchanged for 'intercultural competence' and now I think it is mainly about putting the individual before the culture. Difficult issue! I took part in a course on cultural competence at the Board of Migration in perhaps in 2009. It was called *The Meetings of Culture*. It was mainly about honor violence." Concerning FGM, Sara Johnsdotter underlined that terminology and law has been politicized. "In a vain effort to bring a case to prosecution, legal borders are crossed in an unacceptable way when it comes to the rights of citizens."

Crime, punishment and laws have increasingly become topics through which an 'us' is produced and mobilized against an imagined 'other'. In the words of legal scholar Mosa Sayed in an email: "In today's legal and political situation it would be suicide to call on 'culture' in trials." 'Culture' has increasingly been used, both implicitly and explicitly, in public debates, not only by demagogues on the far right and racists, but also by mainstream opinion-makers. Generally speaking, anthropologists and other 'cultural experts' have been against tapping into it, or becoming part of that discourse.[23] Such an ambivalence is expressed by many other 'cultural experts' (e.g., Good 2008; Bouillier 2011; Holden 2011, 2019a), indicating a reluctance to reduce complexity for the sake of clarity. However, the concept of cultural expertise does not plead for the use of culture in trials but wants to account for the use of socio-anthropological knowledge as a support to the administration of justice (Holden 2019b). The cases mentioned by this paper in fact confirm the relative frequency of the use of cultural expertise even in Sweden, in spite of the novelty of its conceptualization.

In conclusion, the widespread reluctance among anthropologists to use the term 'culture' in a way that counteracts populism discloses a dangerous ambivalence that may also result in the incapacity or unwillingness to actually take a stand. Swedish cultural experts have a long history of being entwined with the state. This is changing, but more debate is needed to develop the roles of such experts (see Mestre i Mestre and Johnsdotter 2019, p. 106).

---

[23] A twist to the expert role of Roma witness ethnologist Arnstberg, and the anthropologist Kajsa Ekholm Friedman, is that in the last decade, both have become closely associated with right-wing ideas about the need to protect Sweden from multiculturalism and cultural diversity.

Perhaps cultural experts, according to the broad definition suggested by Holden, could look more closely at the nuanced argumentation of legal scholars to find support for managing difference within a legal system where equality and the protection of the weaker party has to be maintained. Aylet Shachar's (2014) discussion on culture as a *shield* or a *sword* in civil law opens up for a way to be sensitive to context, without denying the conflicts inherent in cultural claims. Meanwhile, Lernestedt (2010, 2014) encourages scrutiny of the *content* of the yardsticks we use in the legal system. The Swedish state, which is quite blind to its multicultural history, should not be blind to justice. In Sweden, an alliance—or even a simple conversation—between cultural experts concerned with litigation, and legal scholars interested in the expertise of such persons, could be a first step towards fruitful interdisciplinary research and practical action.

Funding: This essay was first presented at the EURO-EXPERT conference held in Oxford on the 3rd and 4th July 2018 and has benefitted from funds from EURO-EXPERT, ERC funded project 681814 led by Livia Holden, the Principal Investigator.

Acknowledgments: I would like to thank all the colleagues and experts named in this text who helped me with material. Without their interest and support, this article could not have been written.

Conflicts of Interest: The author declares no conflict of interest.

References

Beach, Hugh. 1981. *Reindeer-Herd Management in Transition. The Case of Tuorpon Saameby in Northern Sweden*. Uppsala: Uppsala Studies in Cultural Anthropology.

Bouillier, Véronique. 2011. French law courts and South Asian litigants. In *Cultural Expertise and Litigation*. Edited by Livia Holden. Milton Park: Routledge, pp. 53–70.

Dagens Nyheter. 2014. Mörkertalet är jättestort. *Dagens Nyheter*. March 26. Available online: https://www.dn.se/nyheter/sverige/morkertalet-ar-jattestort/ (accessed on 15 September 2019).

Dagens Nyheter. 2015. DN Debatt, 2015. Rasbiologiskt språkbruk i statens rättsprocess mot sameby. *Dagens Nyheter*. June 11. Available online: https://www.dn.se/debatt/rasbiologiskt-sprakbruk-i-statens-rattsprocess-mot-sameby/ (accessed on 15 September 2019).

Ds. 2014. *Den mörka och okända historien. Vitbok om övergrepp och kränkningar av romer under 1900-talet*. Arbetsmarknadsdepartementet: p. 8. Available online: https://www.regeringen.se/rattsliga-dokument/departementsserien-och-promemorior/2014/03/ds-20148/ (accessed on 15 September 2019).

Good, Anthony. 2006. *Anthropology and Expertise in Asylum Courts*. Abingdon: Routledge.

Good, Anthony. 2008. Cultural evidence in courts of law. *Journal of the Royal Anthropological Institute* 14: S47–S60. [CrossRef]

Government Offices of Sweden. 2007. National Minorities and Minority Languages. Available online: https://www.government.se/49b72e/contentassets/bb53f1cff8504c5db61fb96168e728be/national-minorities-and-minority-languages (accessed on 21 March 2019).

Holden, Livia, ed. 2011. Introduction. In *Cultural Expertise and Litigation*. Milton Park: Routledge, pp. 1–10.

Holden, Livia, ed. 2019a. *Cultural Expertise and Socio-Legal Studies*. Studies in Law, Politics, and Society. Bingley: Emerald.

Holden, Livia, ed. 2019b. Beyond Anthropological Expert Witnessing: Toward an Integrated Definition of Cultural Expertise. In *Cultural Expertise and Socio-Legal Studies*. Studies in Law, Politics, and Society. Bingley: Emerald, pp. 181–204.

Jahreskog, Birgitta. 1982. *The Sami National Minority in Sweden*. Stockholm: Almqvist & Wiksell International for The Legal Rights Foundation.

Johnsdotter, Sara. 2008a. Ali och den svenska rättvisan: Det första könsstympningsmålet. Malmö: Egalité.

Johnsdotter, Sara. 2008b. Popular notions of FGC in Sweden: The case of Ali Elm. *Finnish Journal of Ethnicity and Migration* 3: 74–82.

Lernestedt, Claes. 2010. *Dit och tillbaka igen. Om individ och struktur i straffrätten*. Uppsala: Iustus förlag.

Lernestedt, Claes. 2014. Criminal law and 'culture'. In *Criminal Law and Cultural Diversity*. Edited by Will Kymlicka, Claes Lernestedt and Matt Matravers. Oxford: Oxford University Press, pp. 15–46.

Lundmark, Lennart. 2006. *Samernas Skatteland I Norr- och Västerbotten under 300 År*. Stockholm: Institutet för Rättshistorisk Forskning.

Mestre i Mestre, Ruth, M., and Sara Johnsdotter. 2019. Court cases, cultural expertise, and 'female genital mutilation' in Europe. *Studies in Law, Politics, and Society* 78: 95–113.

Mörkenstam, Ulf. 1999. *Om "Lapparnes privilegier": Föreställningar om samiskhet i svensk samepolitik 1883–1997*. Stockholm: Stockholms Universitet.

Mörkenstam, Ulf. 2002. Bilden av den andra i svensk samepolitik. In *Svenska Värderingar?* Edited by Peter Hallberg and Claes Lernestedt. Stockholm: Carlsson Bokförlag, pp. 49–71.

Nafstad, Ida. 2016. Gypsy law—The non-state normative orders of Roma: Scholarly debates and the Scandinavian knowledge chasm. *The Journal of Legal Pluralism and Unofficial Law* 48: 92–109. [CrossRef]

Olgaç Rodell, Christina. 2006. *Den romska minoriteten i majoritetssamhällets skola: från hot till möjlighet*. Stockholm: HLS förlag.

Renteln, Alison. 2004. *The Cultural Defence*. Oxford: Oxford University Press.

Runcis, Maija. 1998. *Steriliseringar i folkhemmet*. Stockholm: Ordfront.

SCB. 2018. Utländska medborgare i Sverige. Available online: https://www.scb.se/hitta-statistik/sverige-i-siffror/manniskorna-i-sverige/utlandska-medborgare-i-sverige/ (accessed on 21 March 2019).

Shachar, Aylet. 2014. Family matters: Is there room for 'culture' in the clurtroom? In *Criminal Law and Cultural Diversity*. Edited by Will Kymlicka, Claes Lernestedt and Matt Matravers. Oxford: Oxford University Press, pp. 119–52.

SOU. 1996. *Sverige, Framtiden och Mångfalden. Slutbetänkande från Invandrarpolitiska Kommittén*. Stockholm: Fritze, p. 55.

Svanberg, Ingvar, and Mattias Tydén. 2005. *Tusen år av invandring. En svensk kulturhistoria*, 3rd ed. Stockholm: Dialogos.

Svt Nyheter. 2017. Yaras familj har fått permanent uppehållstillstånd. *Svt Nyheter*, February 26.

© 2019 by the author. Licensee MDPI, Basel, Switzerland. This article is an open access article distributed under the terms and conditions of the Creative Commons Attribution (CC BY) license (http://creativecommons.org/licenses/by/4.0/).

Article

The "Cultural Test" as Cultural Expertise: Evolution of a Legal–Anthropological Tool for Judges

Ilenia Ruggiu

Department of Law, University of Cagliari, 09123 Cagliari, Italy; iruggiu@unica.it

Received: 18 April 2019; Accepted: 31 July 2019; Published: 2 August 2019

Abstract: This paper analyzes the state of cultural expertise in Italy and then focuses on how it can be improved through a kind of cultural expertise that Italian academics, judges, and lawyers are currently debating: the so-called "cultural test". This is a legal test for dealing with culture, which originally emerged as judicial tool in Northern American courts: It consists of a set of pre-established questions that a judge has to answer in order to decide whether or not to accept a cultural claim made by a migrant or by a person that belongs to minority communities. Whereas some questions of the cultural test refer to typical legal balancing between rights, other questions incorporate anthropological knowledge within the trial, requiring the judge to analyze the cultural practice at issue, its historical origin, the importance it has within the community, and other information about which the judge would not be sufficiently knowledgeable without resorting to anthropology. In this sense, the "cultural test" is a form of standardized cultural expertise that helps both the judge and the cultural expert in their tasks. The paper reveals both the arguments against and those in favor of the adoption of the "cultural test" and how they are currently unfolding in the Italian debate.

Keywords: multiculturalism; cultural expertise; cultural test; cultural rights; culture; migration; judiciary

1. Introduction

Law and anthropology exist within diverse epistemological and methodological fields; they have different aims (e.g., descriptive, anthropology/prescriptive, the law) and different ways of dealing with the diversity of human behavior. Nevertheless, the present condition of multicultural societies urges a dialogue between the two disciplines in an effort to elaborate practical tools in which these two different fields can meet. The law needs anthropology to ensure justice. While judges may not have any anthropological training, they nonetheless must judge behaviors rooted in what the present status of knowledge calls "culture". People can go to prison or lose their children simply because legal systems apply the law without an adequate evaluation of the cultural dimension of behavior. People can see their cultural rights (art. 27 of the 1966 International Covenant of Civil and Political Rights) unjustly denied if the cultural dimension of a controversy is not taken into account by the judge.

Thus, in multicultural societies, cultural expertise is becoming increasingly important as a way of imbuing the law with a kind of knowledge that would otherwise remain inaccessible to judges, lawyers, and other persons involved in a case.

In 1977, Lawrence Rosen—in his seminal article "The anthropologist as expert witness" (Rosen 1977)—analyzed the inclusion of the anthropologist into the trial and the consequences that this could have on judicial reasoning. Since then, cultural expertise has extended its borders and contents. In this paper, I adopt the definition of cultural expertise provided by Livia Holden, according to whom, "cultural expertise is the special knowledge that enables socio-legal scholars, anthropologists, or, more generally speaking, cultural mediators, the so-called 'cultural brokers', to locate and describe relevant facts in light of the particular background of the claimants, litigants or the accused person(s), and in some cases of the victim(s)" (Holden 2011, p. 2).

At the comparative level, each State has different practices on how to introduce this "special knowledge" in the trial, whom to consult as cultural expert, what questions to ask, and what role to recognize to the cultural expertise in the decision. So far, no common model has been adopted, and cultural expertise takes on several forms, which I suggest classifying as follows in the Italian context: professional/nonprofessional, public/private, and case-by-case/standardized.

"Professional" cultural expertise is that performed by a qualified anthropologist or other professional (e.g., ethnopsychologist, historian, academic) who is an expert of the cultural practice[1] emerging in a trial. In this case, the cultural expert is a professional figure, not necessarily belonging to the cultural group, who has studied the practice through fieldwork or books. "Nonprofessional" expertise can be said to be that performed by an institution of that cultural group (e.g., embassy, consulate, government, prefecture, mayor, rabbi, imam, cultural association) or by a lay person (e.g., a *quisque de populo*—man in the street member of that group who is heard as a witness). In this case, the special knowledge/cultural expertise comes directly from a member of the group: The lay/nonprofessional cultural expert is, in fact, capable of explaining the meaning of the cultural practice as they belong to that culture. It is worth pointing out that such definition is unbiased by any intention to look down upon the "lay expert".

"Public" cultural expertise is that requested by the judge in the exercise of their jurisdictional function, and paid using public money, whereas "private" cultural expertise is that which the lawyer introduces in the proceedings of their own motion, by identifying a cultural expert. In this case, the defendant bears the costs. Generally, public cultural expertise requires the cultural expert to be a professional, such as an anthropologist, an ethnopsychologist, etc., whereas private cultural expertise can be provided also by lay experts like embassies, prefectures, etc.

Cultural expertise can be either on a "case-by-case" basis, when an individual cultural expert is consulted for each proceeding and without a pre-established matrix of questions, or it can be "standardized" expertise when there is a fixed procedural tool to use (e.g., handbooks of cultural practices; database of cultural expertise to be consulted by judges; legal tests for dealing with culture).

Although the case-by-case approach may be an appropriate way to deal with the cultural background of facts and people, and it has the indubitable advantage of permitting a more tailored approach to the nuances of each cultural dimension, in practice, it also presents some flaws. It may happen, in fact, that, not having a systematic judicial method to understand the context of the facts, some judges fail to call any cultural expert at all; it may happen that judges ask certain questions and omit others, thus failing to acquire some relevant anthropological information; it may happen that the weight given to certain elements is higher in a case than in another, causing uncertainty; or even that anthropologists, called as experts, without any matrix, might elaborate detailed reports on the cultural dimension of a controversy that do not always respond to what the judge needs.

This paper goes beyond the case-by-case approach that so far is the most widespread in Italy and Europe and argues for the need to reflect on a more structured and standardized way to approach the role of the cultural expertise within cultural disputes. In order to pursue this aim, the paper analyzes a case study: the Italian one. After briefly reconstructing how cultural expertise works in Italy, this paper tackles the present practical challenges connected to cultural expertise in the trial by suggesting the adoption of a legal tool: the so-called "cultural test", which can be used both by judges and by anthropologists. This tool has been known in the legal language as "cultural test" since

---

[1] Far from the intention of essentializing groups and attributing them a static feature, as cultures are dynamic and become embodied in different ways according to different individuals within the group and their movements in space and time, in this paper, I chose to use the concept of "cultural practice" because in the dialogue between the law and anthropology, it appears still very useful for the following reasons. Firstly, the judge has to face a single practice/action/behavior relevant for the law and deliver a judgement with regard to it. Secondly, I recognize that the law needs the concept of "cultural practice" as a tool to give substance to cultural rights internationally recognized as human rights. I invite the reader to approach the concept of "cultural practice" as comprehensive of semantic fields, actions, world-view, beliefs, customs, ideologies, collective memories, and narratives.

1996, when the Canadian Supreme Court created it with the aim to define the conditions to recognize the First Nations' aboriginal rights protected in Section 35 of the Constitution Act, 1982. Actually, because the "cultural test" is a tool designed by jurists, a more appropriate referential terminology might be: "a legal test for dealing with culture". Nevertheless, scholars adopted this judicial wording thereafter (Dundes Renteln 2004; Eisenberg 2009; Dore 2016; Basile 2017; Ruggiu 2019), and this paper uses the common terminology of the cultural test with the caveat that "cultural" does not mean that the test necessarily reflects the view of anthropology on culture. This tool, already used in some jurisdictions in Canada and the United States, although in ways that are not regarded as satisfactory (Borrows 1997–1998), is currently being debated in Italy by judges, lawyers, and legal academics.

The paper argues that the cultural test could become a useful tool in the hands of the "anthropologist judge". By this expression, I mean "any judge who may find herself facing different cultural practices and who decides (on her own initiative) or is induced (by the lawyer) to confront the concept of culture, either in civil, criminal, or administrative jurisdictions and in trial, appeal or supreme courts" (Ruggiu 2019, p. xvii.) The cultural test is addressed as a tool to guarantee the cultural rights of migrants, which are internationally guaranteed. In fact, the precondition to cultural rights is the right to present a cultural defense (Dundes Renteln 2002, p. 199) but benefitting from a guide that enables the judges to perform, with the help of anthropology, an accurate analysis of the elements at stake.

This paper analyzes a specific cultural test that I have elaborated by gathering the most persuasive and recurring *topos*[2] that Western judges use when they settle a case in which the cultural background of facts and people is relevant (Ruggiu 2019).

By looking into the Italian debate, the article aims to provide more general suggestions useful at a comparative level on how judges can be guided in incorporating anthropological knowledge into the trial through the cultural test.

2. The Present State of Cultural Expertise in Italy

In Italy, cultural expertise practice is not systematically used, but there are many occurrences and varieties. When used, cultural expertise can be both professional and nonprofessional, public and private, written and oral and is so far provided on a case-by-case basis.

The lack of request for anthropologists in juridical fields combines, in Italy, with a lack of bureaucratic structuring of anthropology. Anthropologists are not organized in a state board from which the judge can select experts, as happens with engineers, doctors, psychologists, and other technical experts falling within more established and recognized categories (Ciccozzi and Decarli 2019, pp. 36–38). The Italian Legislature has not yet addressed the creation of a state board for cultural experts in the context of multicultural disputes. The only intervention so far, with a view to setting up national professional rolls of anthropologists, is represented by Law 22 July 2014, no. 110 "*Amendment to the Code of Cultural Heritage and Landscape, as per Legislative Decree 22 January 2004, no. 42, in the field of cultural heritage professionals, and establishment of national rolls of the aforementioned professionals*". This law introduces art. 9 *bis* to the Code of Cultural Heritage and Landscape enacted in 2004, envisaging the setting up of national professional rolls of anthropologists and of a new professional category called demo-ethno-anthropologist. Both profiles will be involved in the protection of cultural heritage, namely, in archaeological excavation sites or museums, but not in the issues connected with multiculturalism. A nationwide board of anthropologists to be involved in multicultural disputes would facilitate the work of the lawyers and judges, as they would have a list, with associated CVs, from which to select the name of the persons to consult. Many European States share this situation. Furthermore, in Italy, there is neither a national exam to become an anthropologist, like the bar exam for lawyers or the exam to become an architect or a psychologist, nor a national list of anthropologists. Together with a lack

---

[2] With *topos*, I mean, with Aristotle (384-322 B.C.E.), the shared points reached in a discourse on which there is a stable consensus (Aristotle 2012, book 5.) In this case, the discourse is the one going on between judges in search of multicultural justice.

of demand from judges, these are other obstacles to the systematic involvement of anthropologists in the trial as experts in the context of multicultural disputes. In addition, anthropology suffers also the (misplaced) prejudice in favor of "hard sciences" (medicine, engineering), being a social science, and one of the youngest, so it happens that the judge does not think they need to deepen the information concerning the cultural dimension of the case. Therefore, Italian judges often tend to act as a "solo" anthropologist, analyzing the cultural claim or the cultural context autonomously. Sometimes, this task is well performed, as in the case of a young Moroccan child that was trying to reach his uncle living in Rome to whom he had been entrusted by virtue of *kafalah*. The child was stopped in Casablanca because the Italian Government refused the visa, claiming that *kafalah* was not enough to create a family bond. Judge Giacinto Bisogni, drafting the opinion (Italian Supreme Court of Cassation, I civil section, 2 February 2015, no. 1843), engaged in his own research, found documents concerning *kafalah*, and resolved the case in favor of the recognition of this cultural practice, thus allowing the family reunification of the child with his uncle. Although this "anthropologist judge" analyzed accurately the cultural practice, within other proceedings, Italian judges have committed several "anthropological mistakes". Those can be framed either in the category of "blaming culture for bad behaviour" (Volpp 2000)—as when a judge treated rape in Afghanistan as a cultural practice (Giudice Udienza Preliminare-GUP Bologna, 16 November 2006)—or in the category of "exoticism"—as when the Supreme Court of Cassation treated Roma begging as a cultural practice, while Roma people themselves said that it was not a cultural practice (Ruggiu 2016 and infra).

In addition to judges that act as "solo anthropologist", there are also judges that request cultural expertise (Ciccozzi and Decarli 2019), but more frequently, in Italy, cultural expertise enters the trial on request of culturally-sensitive lawyers who gather information on the cultural dimension of the controversy to be presented to the judge. When this happens, we can talk of a form of "private" cultural expertise.

Cultural experts consulted in Italian case law have heterogeneous expertise. Sometimes they appoint anthropologists, as in the Tavarez case (decided by Court of Appeal of Trieste 19 February 2009, op. no. 48), a family law case in which Nicole Tavarez, daughter of Mr. Louis Aneury Tavarez Marte, was declared adoptable as the judge considered the child abandoned. Anthropologist Federica Rossi was asked by Mr. Tavarez's lawyer to draw up a cultural expert witness report. In the document, the anthropologist states: "I answer the questions asked by lawyer Alberto Patrone, of the *forum* of Trieste, concerning the evaluation of the cultural patterns existing in the Caribbean sea and specifically in the Dominican area, which are relevant to understand the facts decided by the Court of Appeal of Trieste, 19 February 2009, op. no. 48". The expert witness report unfolds along eight pages of detailed analysis firstly of the broader cultural, political, and social history of the Dominican area, then of the model of family existing comparatively in the world. The anthropologist concludes by saying that the extended family model existing also in the Dominican area determines different standards of child care in which the child, as Nicole was, is often entrusted to relatives or friends, or even left alone, and that this does not mean lack of care.

Whereas in this case, an anthropologist was consulted, in most cases, Italian lawyers request cultural expertise from other subjects: official institutions of the defendant's country, such as the Consulate, Embassy, and Prefecture or recognized members of the minority which the defendant belongs to. An Indian Consulate's certificate was, for instance, produced by the lawyer of Mr. Singh, an Indian citizen and member of the Sikh religion, reported to the police for carrying illegal weapons while shopping in a supermarket in Cremona. Along with the traditional clothes and turban, the man was wearing the *kirpan*. The *Trial Court of Cremona*, 19 February 2009, no. 15 stated the reasons, reporting in its opinion excerpts from the Indian Consulate's certificate: "in accordance with what is known based on the documents produced by the defence ... the symbols of (the Sikh) religion are: the *Khanda*, symbol of the *Khalsa*, that is the Sikh community, which consists of a central sword (symbol of faith in God) and two crossed swords (symbol of spiritual and temporal power); the *Khanga* (comb), a symbol of personal care of the person as a creature of God; the *Kirpan* (dagger), a symbol of resistance to evil; the *Kara* (metal bracelet that recalls the principle of non-stealing and also has a balancing function of the iron in the human body) as a sign of unity with God and, finally, the beard and uncut hair, a sign of acceptance of God's will, as the natural will of God is followed. In particular, the follower of the Sikh religion should always carry the *kirpan*, as well as the turban. And this is also expressly confirmed, in a similar case, by the Consulate General of India (see the certificate of 21 June 2001, produced by the defence) which indicates how the Indian Sikh is 'forced', and does not merely have an option, 'for religious reasons to always carry a turban and *kirpan* (small dagger) as required by Sikhism'". After these assessments, the judge acquitted the Sikh for having exercised freedom of religion.

In another case of an Albanian father who kissed his son's genitals, as a form of "homage to the penis" (John et al. 1991) cultural practice, the lawyer presented a statement from the Prefect of Vlore, Albania. This cultural expertise stated that it was common in that area to caress the penis of the child to celebrate "the glory of prosperity" and the happiness for having a male child. This case was brought as a result of the report made by two teachers of an Albanian child who had overheard a conversation between the child and another five-year-old. The latter was reportedly saying: "Yesterday I made all my family laugh by running naked in the house", to which the Albanian child answered: "And my father sucked mine [*penis*]". Requested by the teachers to explain what he meant, the Albanian child mimed the act, by putting a teaspoon in his mouth and moving it up and down: "like that, like a feeding bottle". The teachers reported the case to a judge who ordered to place secret video cameras in the Albanian family's home. The video cameras filmed two episodes in which the father sucked his son's penis; the child's mother was present on one of the occasions. The father and the mother of the child were prosecuted based on such evidence with the charge of sexual abuse. The court of first instance (Tribunale di Reggio Emilia, 21 November 2012) stated the reasons by saying that, although the gesture was clearly sexual according to the Italian criminal code, the father lacked sexual intention since the behavior was culturally motivated based on a tradition of rural Albania (as it was an expression of affection). The Court of Appeal (Corte d'Appello di Bologna, 9 April 2017) upheld the decision, adding that the conduct could not even be considered a crime because "it was a gesture of love and paternal pride toward the male offspring, completely lacking any sexual connotation and conforming to a cultural tradition of rural Albania". The Italian Supreme Court of Cassation (Cassazione, III criminal section, 29 January 2018 no. 29613) annulled the judgment and ordered that a new trial take place (in a different section of the Court of Appeal of Bologna) in order to allow for the rights of the child to prevail, since the sucking and kissing of the penis, which is an erogenous zone, is inherently sexual and the cultural defense cannot be used when it affects crucial rights of the child. The Supreme Court of Cassation deemed the document of the Prefecture of Vlore not accurate, as it "was unverified and lacked authentication (as evidenced by the judge of first instance and by the Public Prosecutor who appealed the judgment) and such document simply reported that in some rural areas of Albania a tradition existed, consisting in caressing one's own son's private parts, as a wish for prosperity" not mentioning at all the kissing of the penis. On 16 May 2019, the Court of Appeal of Bologna condemned the man to 2 years and 8 months of prison for the crime of having committed sexual activities with a minor (sec. 609 quarter Italian criminal code). Given the importance of the interests at stake, in this case, a professional and more detailed cultural expertise explaining that the practice of the "homage to penis" of the child (John et al. 1991) is spread in areas of Albania, Afghanistan, Bulgaria, Cambodia, India, Italy, Vietnam, and several others would have been essential. In fact, the cultural practice was completely unknown to the Italian society, where the mass panic toward pedophilia led the teachers to report the father to the police.

In Italy and elsewhere, it may also happen that the lawyer resorts to the cultural defense without substantiating it by means of any cultural expertise, that is, just claiming that the defendant was moved by their enculturation based on what the defendant claims. This generally happens when the defendant belongs to a cultural minority that is already known in Italy, like the Jewish or the Roma (Gypsies) people, or with respect to cultural practices well known internationally (*kafalah*, female genital mutilation, male circumcision). But sometimes, the lack of cultural expertise and the excess of self-confidence by the lawyers and judges in dealing with a cultural practice lead to misunderstandings, as happened in the so-called "begging case", a 2008 Supreme Court of Cassation opinion (Cassazione, V criminal section, 17 September 2008, op. no. 44516) in which the begging practiced by Roma (Gypsies) was (incorrectly) regarded as a cultural practice (Ruggiu 2016). The case concerned a Roma mother who took her child with her when she begged on the streets. The lawyer asked the judge "not to criminalize a thousand-year-old cultural practice" (without previously consulting any Roma people or any anthropologist). The Supreme Court accepted the cultural claim and mitigated the sentence. A few days after the opinion was delivered, the Roma and Sinti association *Federazione Rom e Sinti Insieme* ("Roma and Sinti Together Federation") denied that begging was part of their culture, stating that, conversely, it was a consequence of the decline of that very culture due to urbanization. In response to this incorrect framing of begging as a Roma cultural practice, the Italian debate polarized and in 2009, in the name of children's rights "against culture", the Italian Parliament enacted a new crime ("begging with a child" art. 600 *octies* of the criminal code), with severe penalties and the automatic loss of parental authority for parents who take their children with them to beg.

The heterogeneity of ways in which anthropological knowledge is brought into Italian courts is also reflected at a procedural level. Indeed, in Italy, cultural expertise can be written or oral: It can be formalized in a document and brought to the attention of the judge by the lawyer; or the cultural expert can be a witness expert, summoned by the lawyer to make a statement and answer questions during the trial; a lay person or the same defendant may be subject to oral examination during the trial with regard to the cultural dimension of the conduct at issue.

This is the status quo of cultural expertise in Italy, but it must be pointed out that there is growing debate, particularly between judges and lawyers, with a view to enhancing the dialogue between law and anthropology and to finding ways to incorporate cultural expertise into the trial in a more efficient and systematic manner. Given the present situation of migration in Italy, the issue is becoming urgent.

3. The Urgency of Incorporating Cultural Expertise into the Trial in Italy

Italy can be classified as a recent de facto multicultural country if compared to other countries where migration is a more consolidated phenomenon. Until the 1970s, Italy was a country of emigration, whereas nowadays, the immigrants who permanently live in the country represent 10% of the population: approximately 6 million people out of a total population of 60 million.

Cultural diversity brings new challenges in the domain of justice, similar to those already seen in other de facto or de iure multicultural states, like the United States (Dundes Renteln 2004) and Canada (Eisenberg 2009). Just to make a few examples of recent cases in which the lack of anthropological knowledge led to failing to attain justice, it should be recalled that in Italy, parents lose parental authority over their sons because judges confuse the cultural practice of the "homage to the penis" with pedophile sexual abuse (see *supra* sec. 2), and Sikhs cannot wear the *kirpan* any longer because it is considered a "weapon" and is regarded as a violation of "Western values" (Court of Cassation, I criminal section, 15 May 2017, no. 24084. Italian courts used to acquit Sikhs wearing a kirpan until 2016). Lack of basic anthropological tools—such as "cultural translation", the capacity to adopt the migrants' "point of view", the search for a "cultural equivalent" in the host society—in the hands of judges, lawyers, mayors, social services, teachers, and citizens are causing several cultural misunderstandings that affect the achievement of actual justice.

Italian civil and criminal courts address each cultural dispute with a case-by-case approach. There is no Multicultural Act, no clear rule for the judges on how to use the cultural defense or recognize foreigners' right to culture, since art. 27 of the 1966 International Covenant of Civil and Political Rights (1966) has never been implemented through a law or through an amendment to the Constitution aimed at recognizing multiculturalism.

The problem of incorporating anthropological knowledge into the trial has become particularly urgent after the so-called "migration crisis" (2014–2017). The number of migrants landing on the

Italian coasts brought thousands of applications for asylum or other forms of international protection to the judges' desks. Many of them are based on cultural grounds: people claiming that they need protection from voodoo rituals, black magic, female genital mutilations, "honor killings". Judges and lawyers started to face cultural questions that often the C.O.I. (Country of Origin Information) they were provided with could not help in answering.

The requests for asylum and international protection have led to a transformation in the same structure of the judiciary. In fact, in order to try to expedite and make the analysis of asylum applications more specific and specialized, 26 special migration sections, one for each Court of Appeal, were established by law 13 April 2017 no. 46.

Given this background, the role of cultural expertise becomes increasingly crucial to the justice system in Italy.

The Italian judiciary has realized the importance of tackling the challenges of multiculturalism. The Italian Supreme Court of Cassation organized a Conference on 2–3 October 2015, at its venue in Rome, on *Multiculturalism and the Courts*, nationally broadcasted on the radio station www.radioradicale.it, in which the judges reflected on the possible tools to be adopted for the solution of multicultural disputes. In March 2018 and 2019, the Italian School for the Judiciary (*Scuola Italiana di Magistratura*) organized at its venue in Scandicci-Florence a three-day course on the subject "Multiculturalism and criminal law" with the participation of a hundred of judges, in which topics such as the role of the "anthropologist judge" (2018) and the "cultural test in theory and practice" (2019) were discussed. In May 2017, the "Observatory on Justice, Transcultural Dialogues and International Protection" (hereinafter, the Observatory on Transcultural Dialogues or the Observatory) was established with the task of drawing up a protocol and guidelines for Italian judges and lawyers on how to solve multicultural disputes. The Observatory is a spontaneous organization based on a model (Observatories on Civil Justice) forged in the 1990s by judge Carlo Maria Verardi, who had the idea of bringing judges and lawyers together to discuss new issues before actual litigation handled by lawyers and judges in court. The task of the existing Observatories is to elaborate protocols and guidelines.[3] Although those are nonbinding, they are informally used in many courts in Italy. The Observatory on Transcultural Dialogues consists of about twenty judges, twenty lawyers, and ten academicians, coming mainly from the school of law. The organization is also open to anthropologists and ethnopsychologists as well as stakeholders, such as migrants' organizations. The Observatory is coordinated by Giacinto Bisogni, judge of the Italian Supreme Court of Cassation, and Paola Lovati, attorney in Milan.

Among other tasks, this Observatory decided to focus on the legal tool known as the "cultural test" in order to analyze how judges and lawyers can benefit from the use of this tool. In the following sections, I analyze this legal tool for dealing with culture as a sort of new form of cultural expertise and describe the current debate around it.

4. The "Cultural Test" as a Form of Cultural Expertise

What is a cultural test? This expression refers to a set of pre-established questions a judge has to answer in order to decide whether or not to accept a cultural claim made by a migrant or members of cultural minorities. The cultural test is a legal tool created by judges and used at the judicial level comparatively. In fact, in order to decide whether or not to accept cultural and religious claims, several judges (the Canadian Supreme Court, the US Supreme Court, the UN Committee of Human Rights) have elaborated so-called "religious tests" and "cultural tests". The first "religious test" was created in the US in 1963 in the Supreme Court opinion *Sherbert v. Verner* (1963), 374 U.S. 398; the first "cultural test" was created in Canada in 1996 in the Supreme Court opinion *R. v. Van Der Peet* [1996], 2 S.C.R. 507.

---

[3] http://milanosservatorio.it/vista-dellassemblea-nazionale-degli-osservatori-reggio-emilia-del-prossimo-fine-settimana-pubblichiamo-la-seconda-scheda-preparatoria-altro-materiale-del-gruppo-lavoro-giustizia-dialogh/.

The US religious test asks the following questions: Which is the religious practice (detailed description)? Is the subject sincere? Is there a substantial burden over a mandatory practice? Is there a State's compelling interest to limit the practice?

The Canadian cultural test asks the following questions: Which is the cultural practice (detailed description)? Is the practice "essential and integral" to the cultural survival of the group? Is the practice "distinctive" from other majority practices? Did the practice exist prior to contact with Europeans (pre-contact test)?

While some questions of the existing cultural tests refer to the typical legal balancing between rights, other questions try to incorporate expertise about culture within the trial, requiring the judge to analyze the cultural practice at issue, its historical origin, and the importance it has within the community, recognizing that the judge would not be sufficiently knowledgeable without resorting to anthropology. For instance, the fact that the judge is obliged to provide a detailed description of the cultural practice at stake by both the abovementioned tests ensures that they do not miss crucial cultural information in deciding the case and that they have to consult an anthropologist to answer the test question.

Some existing cultural tests present old-fashioned visions of cultures or are incomplete with regard to the questions to be asked. The North American tests have been elaborated by judges, under the contingency of their legal systems, and without any consultancy with anthropologists. For instance, the question "did the practice exist prior to contact with Europeans?", included in the Canadian cultural test, has been heavily criticized for freezing aboriginal groups in time (Borrows 1997–1998), against all the contemporary ideas of culture as a dynamic system elaborated by anthropology.

Despite some potential limitations (*infra* sec. 6), the idea of a "cultural test" is worthy of being explored, as it could be a way of introducing on stable terms the cultural expertise into the trial, making sure that crucial anthropology-relevant questions are raised when facing a multicultural dispute.

Comparatively, strong interest in the tool of the cultural test has been shown by several legal scholars who, whilst criticizing existing judicial cultural tests, have put forward their version of a cultural test that can guide judges, lawyers and anthropologists in approaching a cultural dispute (Dundes Renteln 2004, p. 207; Eisenberg 2009, p. 12; De Maglie 2010, pp. 253–60; Dore 2016, p. 552; Basile 2017, pp. 131–34; Ruggiu 2019, pp. 143–201.) The idea of adopting a cultural test is gaining momentum between both legal scholars and practitioners who feel the need to put an end to the random approach to culture in the context of multicultural disputes. The Italian Supreme Court in 2018 referred to some elements suggested by Fabio Basile (2017, pp. 131–34), an Italian professor of criminal law, as important in assessing a cultural claim. The Italian Supreme Court of Cassation, III criminal section, 29 January 2018 no. 29613 opinion reads: "in order to evaluate the impact that the cultural matrix has on the awareness of the agent, it will be useful, as suggested by the most recent academic legal theory [*scholars*], to evaluate *the nature of the cultural provision* to comply with which the crime was committed, whether of *a religious or legal nature* (as would happen if the cultural rule matched a corresponding legal rule in force in the legal system of the immigrant's country of origin, since in the latter case the awareness of the unlawfulness of the conduct, and therefore the culpability concerning the committed fact would be relevant), and [*evaluate*] *whether the cultural norm is binding* (if respected in a homogeneous way by all the members of the cultural group or, rather, obsolete and not widespread also in that context). Ultimately, the *extent of the integration* of the immigrant in the culture and social fabric of the country of destination, and the extent of *persistent adherence to the culture of origin* (an aspect which is relatively independent of the time spent in the host country) will also be *relevant factors to assess*." Personally, I do not consider this embryonic cultural test to be complete, but I consider this opinion relevant since, for the first time, the Italian Supreme Court mentioned the need of fixed elements to construct the judicial evaluation. The next step, in my opinion, should be to refine this embryo of a cultural test in order to ensure that a permanent and complete form of standardized cultural expertise is introduced into the trial. The following sections show how Italian judges are tackling this challenge.

5. A Proposal of "Cultural Test" Debated in Italy

In order to stop the unpredictable and heterogeneous way in which Italian judges approach multicultural disputes, judges, lawyers and legal scholars within the Observatory on Transcultural Dialogues are discussing the possibility of adopting a cultural test as a guideline in stating the reasons of judgements and opinions. In perspective, other jurisdictions may also use this tool comparatively, as it gathers the most persuasive questions already adopted by judges (and anthropologists) in the trial.

The test currently debated at the Observatory on Transcultural dialogues and during training courses with Italian judges (e.g., Superior School of the Judiciary, Scandicci, 14 March 2019 course on Multiculturalism and criminal law) still needs a deeper discussion with a wider community of anthropologists, in Italy and internationally, as so far, it is a legal instrument discussed mainly among jurists. So far, it represents an attempt, from part of the law, to incorporate cultural expertise within the trial, and in this sense, it can be considered a starting point of a possible dialogue between the law and anthropology.

The cultural test currently debated at the Observatory on Transcultural dialogues consists of the following questions:

1. Does the matter fall within the *category of culture*?
2. *Describe* the cultural practice and the group.
3. Relate and link the practice with the broader cultural system/web of significances.
4. Is the practice *essential* (to the group's survival), *compulsory* or *optional*?
5. Is the practice *shared* or *contested* within the group?
6. Is the group *vulnerable* within a society? Is it discriminated against?
7. How would a *reasonable person in that group* behave in the same circumstances?
8. Is the subject *sincere, honest* and *consistent* in claiming the cultural practice?
9. Is there a *cultural equivalent*, a similar or comparable practice, in the majority culture?
10. Is the practice *harmful*? Is the harm irreparable?
11. Does the practice perpetuate *patriarchy*?
12. What is the impact of the practice on the culture and value system of the *majority*?
13. What positive reasons support the minority following that practice? Is the practice an *equally valuable and meaningful life choice*?

These questions, intertwined and complementing each other, can be grouped into a triadic structure comprising the objective, subjective, and relational parts of the test.

1. *Objective evaluation.* The first group of questions (#1–6) aims to investigate the conditions for the recognition of a cultural practice by examining its objective characteristics. In this stage, the cultural expert's contribution is essential as the law provides no answer to those questions, except for question 6, which the judge can answer by observing the social context in order to check if the minority is welcomed or discriminated against.
2. *Subjective evaluation.* The second set of questions in the proposed test (#7–8) focuses on the relationship between culture and its actual manifestation in different personal identities. This subjective investigation is needed to verify that the litigants do not use cultural arguments as a mere tactical tool, as well as to give the judge a more accurate measure of the interests involved in the dispute. In this stage, factual evidence from witnesses is essential. The help of a cultural expert is also necessary in this stage, especially for question 7.
3. *Relational evaluation.* The test is completed with a relational assessment of the conflict (questions #9–13). The fact that the objective (there is a cultural practice, with a certain extent of obligation) and subjective (the person sincerely adheres to that practice, which is a constituent part of their identity) requirements are met does not mean that the legal response must necessarily be recognition. In fact, there is the need to consider cultural needs compared with those of others,

in this case of the majority of the society. A test that is limited to the mere objective assessment betrays the particularity of law as a science of settlement of social conflict. In this relational part of the test, question 9 calls for the help of an anthropologist. Only a cultural expert, in fact, is able to proceed to the "cultural translation" of behavior explaining its value and significance in the two different "webs of significances" (Geertz 1973, p. 5), of the majority and the minority.

The discussion regarding the possibility of adopting this legal test for dealing with culture is still ongoing within the Observatory and the Italian Judiciary, but it is already possible to identify the main arguments against and in favor of its adoption.

6. Arguments against the Adoption of the "Cultural Test"

Without any order of importance, the following criticisms towards the adoption of the "cultural test" can be foreseen.

A first criticism is that it appears to be a "legal transplant" from common law systems that could alter the way in which, in Italy, judges state the reasons of judgments. Indeed, whereas Italian judges have the duty to state the reasons of their opinions, they are not subject to fixed rules on how to do this and enjoy discretionary power in this regard, connected to the independence of the Judiciary. Therefore, some perceive the test as a tool that limits the freedom of the judge and their capability to choose the arguments to settle the multicultural dispute. One possible solution to this is that the test remains an element additional to the written opinion. This would mean that the judge takes it into account, albeit without having to state the reasons in such a manner as if they were compulsorily answering the questions of the cultural test. This could be a compromise between a common law tradition and a civil law tradition, which could ensure that judges use homogeneous tools in their reasoning whilst not losing their discretionary power.

A second risk, connected to the first, concerns the lawfulness of the cultural test, until it is introduced in the formal legal system by the legislature. Italian judges (as all democratic judges) give their opinion "in the name of the Italian people", and they are subject only to the law. In Northern America, the US religious test became a law (Religious Freedom Restoration Act-RFRA 1993), but the same is unlikely to happen in Italy, where the legislature tends not to impose on the judiciary tools to state the reason of their opinions. Therefore, some judges foresee an issue of lawfulness in deciding a case following such method. Again, the solution to this problem—discussed within the Observatory on Transcultural Dialogues—could be that the test does not become a compulsory tool but is used as a form of guideline, of best practice for the judges. Another solution is that the test starts to be used by the Supreme Court of Cassation in its decisions as the proper way to state the reasons in the context of a cultural case. In this way, the cultural test could become a self-adopted judicial tool.

A fourth possible risk of adopting the cultural test is that of essentializing groups (Ricca 2005). Within the Observatory, for instance, the anthropologist Stefania Spada observes that cultures are dynamic and embodied in a different way: The test, risking to proceed according to a reifying and reductionist logic, would not cover the multiple subjective declinations of cultural knowledge and would not be able to understand the contextual and particular differences of individuals. The knot that raises criticality is precisely the way to elaborate the concept of culture. Culture is co-produced at both intersubjective and group level, in the different spaces/places in which the subject is embedded; the dynamics of co-production also proceed in a different way according to the contexts they originate from or the situations that host the contact with "cultural otherness" (migratory contexts, post-colonial spaces, etc.). In "handling the cultural dimension", it would therefore be appropriate to look at life stories and material conditions of existence to avoid misunderstandings arising from an ethnocentric reading, implemented through categories established in a unilateral way and often essentialized.

There is also the risk that cultural groups submit cultural claims tailored to the questions of the test, thus distorting their culture, and even constructing false cultural claims. According to this view, a case-by-case approach should be preferred, as it would help to avoid that the litigants construct a case around the issues highlighted in the test that they know the judge would take into consideration.

A response to those criticisms comes from the urgency to avoid cultural injustice by assessing cultural aspects within the trial's features and constraints. While it is important not to essentialize an individual or stereotyping a group, cultural practices and behaviors do, in fact, exist. Actually, the judge is under a duty to decide the case. In contrast to the legislature, which is free to decide to leave multicultural conflicts without a legal framework, the judiciary cannot say *"non liquet"*, "I do not know how to solve this case". Judges must provide a solution, and the more expertise about the cultural dimension of that behavior relevant for the law they have, the better they may serve justice. One could say that this expertise could enter the trial case-by-case, but in practice, if the judges are not guided in a field that is often unknown to them, they may completely ignore that cultural aspects are at stake. The presence of a test which has several questions to be answered, with the help of an anthropologist, can avoid this risk.

A second response to the anti-essentialist criticism is that sometimes, essentialism can be the lesser evil. Particularly in criminal law and family laws, persons face heavy charges: Parents that kiss their sons in the penis as a kind of cuddle, because in their culture this is an admitted behavior, risk going to jail for sexual abuse; parents that practice cupping (a folk medicine) on their children risk going to jail for the crime of assault and battery of a minor. Those persons risk having their children given to foster care, their family broken, their life destroyed. I believe it is a lesser evil to run the risk that Italian society essentialize Albanian fathers as "fathers who kiss their baby's penis" rather than that an Albanian father goes to jail. Anti-essentialism was born out of anticolonial discourse. We should be careful it does not become a way to indirectly perpetuate injustice. We live in an age of mass migration. Many of the six million persons who have immigrated to Italy had to leave their countries for injustices connected to the neocolonial political structure of the world (e.g., capitalist wars, globalization, climate change). If to the trauma of having to leave their home-country, we add the trauma of having their cultural rights ignored, we would disadvantage migrant minorities. In this context, the concept of a "strategic essentialism" (Spivak 1996) was born. According to strategic essentialists, whilst essentialism and reification of cultures and other vulnerable groups (Stone 2004) should be avoided as descriptively inaccurate, it can be politically promoted as a tool to obtain political results in favor of the group. Of course, if the cultural dimension of the behavior is not genuine, the claim does not deserve recognition: The cultural test precisely provides the questions to avoid false claims.

A fifth adverse argument against the test is that the questions of the test are imbued with ethnocentrism. The thirteen questions designed as relevant, in fact, may not necessarily coincide with the ones that are significant to the litigant: Being constrained in the straitjacket of a legal test, the litigant might silent facets and items relevant and truly important for him/her. Furthermore, the approach to knowledge based on cultural models—as the cultural test might appear—is antithetical to the current anthropological method. The test might seem to appeal to anthropological knowledge, but actually it could limit it, as in anthropology, the study of culture does not proceed by "practices" but, rather, by semantic fields, discourses about practices, ideologies, memories, and politics.

But as already discussed, the "cultural test" should be intended as a guideline containing the essential questions to ask when facing a cultural dispute: It should not be intended as closed and fixed. Actually, some of its questions are already built in a broad way to allow the anthropologist who answers them to describe accurately all the aspects involved. For instance, questions 2 and 3 ask to describe the cultural dimensions of facts at stake and then to insert it within the broader web of significance. In this part, the anthropologist can detail more relevant aspects emerging from fieldwork explaining the semantic fields, discourses about the practice, ideologies, memories, and politics in which the behavior, belief, or word view can be understood. As explained before, the alternative is to risk failing to consider any cultural aspects of the controversy at all.

Other criticisms concern single questions within the cultural test. For instance, asking if the practice is essential, compulsory or optional (question no. 4) might seem inaccurate from an anthropological point of view, as anthropologists are disinclined to classify practices on the basis of their binding nature.

Here, we can see the difficulty of the dialogue between two sciences with different epistemological and methodological horizons. In fact, this question is very important with regard to the legal balancing that the judge has to carry out and is also one *topos* of multicultural case law nowadays (Ruggiu 2019, p. 161).

Another question which needs a deeper discussion with anthropologists is that (no. 7) concerning the behavior of the reasonable person within the group, as different individuals embody culture in different ways, whilst lawyers and judges need to size up behavior against some parameters in order to understand if the defendant concerned can actually be justified by their cultural rights or not.

7. Arguments in Favor of the Adoption of the "Cultural Test"

The first argument in favor of the adoption of the cultural test is that it provides a clear path to the judge, the lawyers, and the same anthropologist called as expert witness, concerning the questions to address when faced with a cultural dispute. The existence of a test according to which the court is called upon to verify, through a matrix of predetermined questions, the conditions under which to grant recognition to culture is a way that stabilizes cultural expertise within the trial and guarantees that the judge, the lawyers, and the anthropologist do not overlook key questions. Nowadays, multicultural disputes in Italy are resolved within very heterogeneous statements of reasons: Some judges deem it relevant to ascertain whether the cultural practice is compulsory or optional; others, whether or not the cultural practice causes harm. The presence of a grid of predetermined questions that each judge can follow should favor the principle of legal certainty.

A second benefit, which concerns both judges and anthropologists, is that of ensuring conciseness. The test can be a useful tool that guides the same anthropologist with a fixed number of questions. In fact, sometimes, anthropologists tend to draft long cultural witness reports containing information that might be of no interest for the judge. Particularly in a context in which judges are overwhelmed by asylum seekers' requests based on culture, the test can limit the length and comprehensive nature of a cultural expertise, creating an easy-to-read document.

A third benefit of the cultural test is that it may contribute to saving time and consequently guaranteeing a more expedite way to deliver judgements. Knowing what questions to ask when resolving a multicultural dispute avoids delays and doubts for both judges and anthropologists.

A fourth benefit is that of obtaining more clearly reasoned opinions that can favor social coexistence, rather than exacerbate social conflicts and hostility towards minorities. Often the opinions in which the judges were inclined to recognize a form of cultural defense brought about contrast with Italian public opinion because they stated the reasons in a way that was not anthropologically accurate: Saying that Roma beg for culture draws a line between Roma people and Italians, creating an "other" that is far from us and not understandable. By contrast, saying that Roma take their children to beg with them because they do not want to part from their children and they involve them in adults' activities is something that Italians can understand better. Asking to describe the cultural practice at stake in detail (question no. 2) implies that the judge must consult an anthropologist that is able to frame begging in a more accurate way.

Further, identifying the "cultural equivalent" (question no. 9) in the Italian culture would bridge the cultural gap and make the practice more understandable.

8. Other Tools to Go Beyond the Case-by-Case Cultural Expertise

Whilst drafting a protocol and guidelines for Italian judges and lawyers on how to resolve multicultural disputes, the opportunity to provide, together with the tool of the test, also a handbook of the cultural practices is being discussed.

Again, this need felt by the legal systems, might clash with the current anthropology which could see it as an "encyclopedia of cultures", a tool that, again, might essentialize groups and provide a fixed, stereotypical idea of cultures, freezing groups and persons in time and space. The handbook might bring the old colonizers' reports during imperialism back to anthropologists' minds (Holden 2019a, p. 183). I believe that a solution to this criticism could lie in the way in which such a handbook is written. It should not be an "atlas of cultures" but rather a recollection of single cultural practices. If anthropologists are involved, and it is designed in a critical and conscious way, this tool can satisfy the need to incorporate expertise about culture in the trial. In fact, judges need information, and often, the "urgency" and "emergency" of the case cause them to overlook some important cultural information, which a readable easy-to-consult handbook can provide. In this regard, it is interesting to note that some lawyers are autonomously creating their own database of cultural practices that may appear in their cases. For instance, Benedetta Piola Caselli, attorney in Rome, member of the Observatory, who deals constantly with culturally motivated behavior in her legal practice, has contacted the anthropologist Claudia Cavallari in order to prepare a list of the most relevant cultural practices, in particular concerning groups coming from Africa, that the lawyer has faced in her profession.

Written by anthropologists in cooperation with jurists, this tool would provide judges and lawyers with an easy-to-read, nonstereotyped description of the cultural dimension of facts that have so far appeared in courts or that may appear in the future. The presence of a cultural expert is ideal and should always be guaranteed in a trial, but when, for any reason (e.g., lack of available experts, difficulty to find them, cuts to budget to consult experts) judges cannot find one, they can, at least, rely on a tool written and constantly updated by anthropologists that provides crucial information. Something similar already exists in Italy with the "Country of Origin Information" (C.O.I.): reports used in the context of asylum seekers' and international protection cases that list the political situation and persecutions suffered in the home country. Sometimes the C.O.I. includes references to the cultural background of certain practices. The aim of the handbook on cultural practices is broader and consists in providing an accurate description of the cultural dimension of recurrent practices and their roles in order to answer questions from 1 to 5 and no. 9 of the cultural test. This idea was endorsed by the honorary president of the Italian Society of Applied Anthropology, professor Antonino Colajanni, during the training course for judges which took place at the Superior School for Judges on 14 March 2019, Scandicci (Florence).

Another need expressed by Italian judges in this same training course is to know how the case has been decided in the home country: Knowing the legal decision of the cases, they could align their decisions to guarantee, when possible, that the defendant is treated in a similar way as if they were judged in the country of origin. At the moment, there is no project that collects this kind of case law.

The Observatory on Transcultural dialogues showed great interest toward ongoing projects aimed at elaborating other tools that collect in a more stabilized way cultural expertise. The project EURO-EXPERT coordinated by the legal anthropologist Livia Holden at the University of Oxford is elaborating a database on cultural expertise in fifteen European states. Another project coordinated by Marie-Claire Foblets at the Max Planck Institute for social anthropology of Halle (The Max Planck database project on religious and cultural diversity) is elaborating a database on comparative multicultural jurisprudence (Foblets and Renteln 2009). Both projects provide databases that are useful when a judge is resolving similar cases.

All these possible instruments work together for a better justice.

9. Conclusions

In this paper, I have analyzed the current debate on cultural expertise in Italy and supported the importance of going beyond the existing case-by-case cultural expertise, to reach more standardized forms that can guide the judges when resolving a multicultural dispute. Particularly, I have focused on the "cultural test": a legal test for dealing with culture that can be considered as a type of cultural expertise. I have claimed that the cultural test falls within the current broad phenomenology of cultural expertise since, within its thirteen questions and particularly within questions 1–5 and 9, it permits to imbue legal proceedings with knowledge about culture. In fact, when using the cultural test as a guideline to state the reasons of their judgement, the judge has to carry out, with the help of a cultural expert, an anthropological analysis of the cultural dimension of the case.

The "cultural test" tool has been contextualized in light of the state of the art of cultural expertise, and it has been actively compared with other standardized tools.

In Sections 1–3 of this paper, I analyzed the status quo of cultural expertise, showing how cultural expertise can manifest itself in several forms, which I have proposed to classify as follows: professional/nonprofessional, public/private, and case-by-case/standardized. I have noticed that this confirms the need for a more inclusive concept of cultural expertise (Holden 2019a). I have also claimed the urgency to stabilize cultural expertise in Italy in order to avoid cultural misunderstandings such as that which led to the sentencing of Sikhs for wearing the *kirpan*, and of an Albanian father who kissed his son's penis while performing an "homage to the penis" (John et al. 1991) cultural practice.

In Sections 4 and 5, I endorsed the adoption of a new tool to resolve multicultural disputes in Italy: the so-called cultural test. I have described it as a legal tool that can favor the encounter between the law and anthropology and serve as a guide both for judges and cultural experts. The cultural test, in fact, contains some of the most relevant questions that should be asked to ascertain the nature of a cultural practice and to balance the right of the migrant to preserve their culture with other rights.

In Section 6, I discussed the criticisms against the cultural test: the fact that it is transposition of a legal institute not belonging to the Italian judicial tools; the risk it entails of limiting the freedom of the judge in stating the reasons of the judgment or opinion; and the risk of becoming an ethnocentric, essentializing straitjacket that compresses the specificity of each case. In Section 7, I discussed the advantages of using a cultural test: favoring the principle of legal certainty; guaranteeing a more expedite way to deliver judgements; and obtaining more clearly reasoned opinions that can favor social coexistence.

In Section 8, I endorsed the adoption of other tools that can favor the democratization of anthropological knowledge and work alongside the cultural test for a better justice: a handbook on cultural practices, a database on the cultural expertise gathered so far, and a database on the comparative multicultural jurisprudence about cases similar to the one judges are solving.

Despite the epistemological and methodological differences between the law and anthropology, this age of mass migration calls for both jurists and anthropologists to actively contribute to the accomplishment of practical aims and to identify solutions that can help to protect cultural rights of migrants and favor multicultural coexistence. In order to obtain this, I reckon it is important to overcome the case-by-case cultural expertise and to find ways to standardize the latter. There is still a "widespread reluctance of anthropologists to become involved with applied sciences" (Holden 2019b, p. 3) rooted in the "self-reflection" (Holden 2019a, p. 188) going on after the errors of the "colonial anthropology" (Holden 2019a). However, there is also an increasing consciousness about the need to participate in order to ensure a multicultural justice, thereby revaluing the historical role of anthropology in support of subalterns and minorities (Holden 2019c). Jurists at present admit that they cannot tackle multicultural litigation without the support of anthropology, and, by providing cultural expertise, anthropologists answer the call for a better justice. The time is ripe to conceive practical tools that can favor the encounter between anthropology and the law within legal proceedings.

Funding: This special issue is an output of the project titled "Cultural Expertise in Europe: What is it useful for?" (EURO-EXPERT) funded by the European Research Council (ERC) under H2020-EU.1.1. programme (ERC grant agreement no. 681814), Principal Investigator: Livia Holden. This paper was also funded from the European Union's Horizon2020 research and innovation program H2020-DRS-2015, under grant agreement No. 700385 Project CLISEL, "Climate Security with Local Authorities", and by the Swiss State Secretariat for Education, Research and Innovation (SERI) under contract number 16.0038. This paper reflects only the author's view and the Agency is not responsible for any use that may be made of the information it contains. The opinions expressed and arguments employed herein do not necessarily reflect the official views of the EU and the Swiss Government.

Acknowledgments: This paper has been revised by Chiara Rotondi. I thank Livia Holden and the anonymous reviewers for their extremely useful feedbacks.

Conflicts of Interest: The author declares that she is in no situation of conflict of interest.

References

Aristotle. 2012. Topics (Translated by William Adair Pickard-Cambridge). In *The Organon: The Works of Aristotle on Logic*. Edited by Roger Bishop Jones. Scotts Valley: CreateSpace Independent Publishing Platform.

Basile, Fabio. 2017. I reati cd. 'culturalmente motivati' commessi dagli immigrati: (Possibili) soluzioni giurisprudenziali. *Questione Giustizia* 1: 26–135. Available online: http://www.questionegiustizia.it (accessed on 31 July 2019).

Borrows, John. 1997–1998. Frozen rights in Canada: Constitutional interpretation and the trickster. *American Indian Law Review* 22: 37–64. [CrossRef]

Ciccozzi, Antonello, and Giorgia Decarli. 2019. Cultural expertise in Italian courts: Contexts, cases, and issues. *Cultural Expertise and Socio-Legal Studies: Special Issue, Series Studies in Law, Politics, and Society* 78: 35–54.

De Maglie, Cristina. 2010. *I Reati Culturalmente Motivati. Ideologie e Modelli Penali*. Pisa: Edizioni ETS.

Dore, Isaak I. 2016. *Homo Juridicus. Culture as a Normative Order*. Durham: Carolina Academic Press.

Dundes Renteln, Alison. 2002. In defense of culture in the Courtroom. In *Engaging Cultural Differences. The Multicultural Challenge in Liberal Democracies*. Edited by Richard Shweder, Martha Minow and Hazel Rose Markus. New York: Russell Sage Foundation, pp. 194–215.

Dundes Renteln, Alison. 2004. *The Cultural Defense*. Oxford: Oxford University Press.

Eisenberg, Avigail. 2009. *Reasons of Identity. A Normative Guide to the Political and Legal Assessment of Identity Claims*. Oxford: Oxford University Press.

Foblets, Marie Claire, and Alison Dundes Renteln. 2009. *Multicultural Jurisprudence: Comparative Perspectives on the Cultural Defense*. Edited by Marie-Claire Foblets and Alison Dundes Renteln. Oxford: Hart Publishing.

Geertz, Clifford. 1973. *The Interpretation of Cultures*. New York: Basic Books Inc.

Holden, Livia. 2011. *Cultural Expertise and Litigation: Patterns, Conflicts, Narratives*. Edited by Livia Holden. New York and London: Routledge.

Holden, Livia. 2019a. Beyond anthropological expert witnessing: Toward an integrated definition of cultural expertise. *Cultural Expertise and Socio-Legal Studies: Special Issue, Series Studies in Law, Politics, and Society* 78: 181–204.

Holden, Livia. 2019b. Cultural expertise and socio-legal studies: Introduction. *Cultural Expertise and Socio-Legal Studies: Special Issue, Series Studies in Law, Politics, and Society* 78: 1–9.

Holden, Livia. 2019c. Cultural expertise and law: An historical overview. *Law & History Review Cambridge*. forthcoming.

John, Money, K. Swayam Prakasam, and Venkat N. Joshi. 1991. Transcultural Development Sexology: Genital Greeting Versus Child Molestation. *IPT (Institute for Psichological Therapies)* 3: 4. Available online: http://www.ipt-forensics.com/journal/volume3/j3_4_4.htm (accessed on 31 July 2019).

Ricca, Mario. 2005. Intercultural Law, Interdisciplinary Outlines. *Lawyering and Anthropological Expertise in Migration Cases: Before the Courts*. Available online: http://ssrn.com/abstract=2800575 (accessed on 31 July 2019).

Rosen, Lawrence. 1977. The anthropologist as expert witness. *American Anthropologist* 79: 555–78. [CrossRef]

Ruggiu, Ilenia. 2016. Is begging a Roma cultural practice? Answers from the Italian law and anthropology. *Romanì Studies* 26: 31–61. [CrossRef]

Ruggiu, Ilenia. 2019. *Culture and The Judiciary: The Anthropologist Judge*. London: Routledge.

Spivak, Gayatri C. 1996. *The Spivak Reader: Selected Works of Gayati Chakravorty Spivak*. Edited by Donna Landry and Gerald MacLean. New York: Routledge.

Stone, Alison. 2004. Essentialism and Anti-Essentialism in Feminist Philosophy. *The Journal of Moral Philosophy* 1: 135–53. [CrossRef]

Volpp, Leti. 2000. Blaming culture for bad behaviour. *Yale Journal of Law & the Humanities* 12: 89–116.

 © 2019 by the author. Licensee MDPI, Basel, Switzerland. This article is an open access article distributed under the terms and conditions of the Creative Commons Attribution (CC BY) license (http://creativecommons.org/licenses/by/4.0/).

Article

The Bondo Society as a Political Tool: Examining Cultural Expertise in Sierra Leone from 1961 to 2018

Aisha Fofana Ibrahim

Institute for Gender Research and Documentation (INGRADOC), Fourah Bay College, University of Sierra Leone, 00232 Freetown, Sierra Leone; mamaisha@gmail.com

Received: 25 April 2019; Accepted: 30 July 2019; Published: 12 August 2019

Abstract: This paper focuses on the politics of the Bondo—the competition among social groups for an exclusive influence on the National strategy for the reduction of female genital mutilation/cutting (FGM/C). In the first part, this paper shows how the Bondo—a women's only secret society—has become a site of contestation for not only pro- and anti-FGM/C advocates, but also elite male politicians who have, since independence in 1961, continued to use the Bondo space for political gains. The use of the Bondo for political leverage and influence pre-dates independence and is as old as the society itself. The second part of this paper discusses the legitimacy of expertise as central to this debate, in which each group competes to become the leading expert. Thus, even though human rights/choice discourse currently dominates the FGM/C debate, traditional expertise remains valid in the formulation of community by-laws as well as state policies and laws. This can be seen in the recent attempt by the state to develop a National Policy for the Reduction of FGM/C in which the expertise of all three groups was sought. Using data from existing literature and personal interviews, this paper interrogates this contention by describing how the role of cultural experts—especially the Soweis—has been politicized in the stalemate over the enactment of the National Policy for the Reduction of FGC. This paper concludes with considerations about the complexity of Bondo expertise, in which opposing parties use similar arguments to evoke the human rights discourses on women's rights and bodily integrity/autonomy. It argues that a better knowledge of these dynamics as they develop in Sierra Leone and other African countries would be useful to the European jurisdiction.

Keywords: Bondo; FGM/C; National Strategy; cultural expertise; human rights

1. Introduction

In Sierra Leone, secret societies not only offer gendered and cultural spaces but—more importantly—operate as a crucial site of political power, making profound decisions about community wellbeing such as the promulgation of laws and how initiations are carried out (Fanthrope 2006; Pemunta and Tabenyang 2017). The trajectories and nuances of the Bondo—a women's only secret society that practices FGC—can be best interrogated through an understanding of the political economy of the practice. This is because the Bondo is both an economic and political enterprise, with Bondo leaders working hand in hand with traditional male authorities in different political spaces. Bondo leaders are often self-seeking and maximize their utility by participating in political activity for both political and economic gains, as manifested in the role they play in the preparation of girls for marriage to powerful political leaders. Dating back hundreds of years, the society has always been dependent on the male patronage of paramount chiefs and politicians, the majority of whom are members of male secret societies. Male power and control is manifested through the society's symbiotic relationship with the all-male Poro secret society, as well as the Bondo society's location within traditional power structures. At the economic level, the Bondo is arguably an economic enterprise with heads earning their livelihood through fees charged for initiations and other related fines. As Bosire (2012) argues "the debates about FGC are not simply about" "the defence of culture," "they are also about livelihoods" (p. 90).

Unlike in other places, in Sierra Leone, excision takes place within the context of a secret society—the Bondo Society. Excised women and girls automatically become members of the Bondo, which is operated by "powerful" women called 'digba' or 'Sowei' who have consistently laid claim to cultural expertise with regard to the practice. The membership aspect suggests that the society transcends the act of cutting, but yet this cutting is an important aspect of its rituals. According to Bosire (2012), the Bondo is a "repository of gendered knowledge that bequeaths members with privileges and power safeguarded by secrecy" (p. 51). The oath of secrecy used to be so strong that initiates were afraid to openly discuss the procedure—a taboo that no longer prevails. Moreover, as Bosire (2012) further elaborates, "soweis reported that Bondo initiation increasingly involved only the ritual cut and customary Bondo teachings were limited. The commercialization of Bondo initiation has also, in one aspect, had the effect of whittling down the traditional symbolic authority accorded to soweis" (p. 88). There are two main procedures performed in Sierra Leone—sunna, the removal of the hood of the clitoris, with the body of the clitoris remaining intact; and clitoridectomy or excision, which is the removal of the clitoris and all or part of the labia. Bjalkander et al. (2013), from a study that involved genital examinations of women who had undergone the procedure, posit that even though the majority of respondents may have wrongly described the form of cutting experienced, forms of type 1 and 2 continue to be the most prevalent forms of FGM in Sierra Leone. This is to say that other types do exist, but are very rare. Depending on the region and person asked, the procedure is justified on the basis of tradition, religion, rites of passage, health and assurance of virginity before marriage as well as marital fidelity, but with the majority arguing that it is a tradition and culture dealing with rites of passage that should be upheld.

2. The Bondo Society of Sierra Leone

The West African region is home to a number of all-male and all-female secret societies, which continue to play an important role in communal life especially in the rural areas. As Mgbako et al. (2010) explain, "Secret societies have fulfilled a number of philosophical, economic, political, social, religious, and educational functions in their communities throughout history, and they continue to play a significant role in contemporary West Africa" (p. 118). The Sande—traditionally an all-female society—predominates in the Mano River region (Sierra Leone, Liberia and Guinea) and is shrouded in secrecy and female power. Although genital cutting is not uniform across these countries and among ethnic groups, it remains a pre-requisite for membership of the secret societies. Commonly referred to as the Bondo Society in Sierra Leone, initiates of the Bondo take an oath of secrecy and are not allowed to disclose what goes on in the Bondo bush. The consequences of breaking the oath are believed to include an individual and/or family curse and infertility. Non-members are neither allowed into the Bondo bush nor allowed to discuss Bondo affairs or offend a Bondo member.

The Bondo bush—the sacred place for society women—is often located in the forest far away from daily life. This dynamic has changed considerably, with Bondo bushes now springing up in the middle of towns and behind people's backyards. The Bondo is very hierarchical and has a well-defined organizational structure, with a head Sowei and other members in various other positions. Soweis are expected to undergo an intensive 2 to 3-year period of training in how to perform genital cutting and apply medicinal remedies. Soweiship is often hereditary and handed down from generation to generation. For Ahmadu (Sulkin 2009) "the institution itself is synonymous with women's power, their political, economic, reproductive and ritual spheres of influence. Excision, or removal of the external clitoral glans and labia minora, in initiation is a symbolic representation of matriarchal power" (p. 14).

However, the Bondo society has had its own fair share of problems in a modernizing society in which people are progressively accessing information from within and without. On the one hand, it is an institution that contributes to social cohesion in communities by maintaining law and order and, on the other, it is a site of struggle. As Bosire (2012) points out, "the Bondo, like all cultural phenomena, is also a site of social struggle. The acquisition of leadership positions within the Bondo is a process in which some of the inherent tensions and debates and cultural uses of the Bondo, the meanings associated with some Bondo values, and the changing structures of the Bondo are played out. The tensions in the Bondo are partly engendered by the changes that the Bondo is undergoing in contemporary post-war Sierra Leone and in the face of FGC eradication discourse" (pp. 76–77).

The Bondo is embodied in a patriarchal ideology that associates women with the body, and with blood and flesh. As Ahmadu (Sulkin 2009) postulates, "Bondo women elders believe and teach that excision improves sexual pleasure by emphasizing orgasms reached through stimulation of the g-spot, which is said to be more intense and satisfying for an experienced woman. Excision of the protruding clitoris is said to aesthetically and physiologically enhance the appearance of the vulva and facilitate male/female coitus by removing any barrier to complete, full and deep penetration" (p. 16). Over time, women's bodies have been despised, tolerated, and exalted, depending upon the immediate context and prevailing politics. Male desires and politics have been scripted onto the female body and women have unwittingly accepted these scripts (Lee and Sasser-Coen 1996, p. 6). Arguably, the Bondo society of Sierra Leone—in which women believe they yield a particular power, (for they alone perform excisions)—not only perpetuates the use and misuse of the female body, but also male desires and politics.

The Bondo symbolizes a girl's entrance into female fecundity and adult female sexuality and serves as a social marker of movement from being a girl to a woman. The question that has always marked the debate is—does a young woman have to lose a vital organ to make such a move? Moreover, what does it mean to experience such a crucial signifier of womanhood in a society that devalues women, especially when this devaluation occurs through cultural scripts associated with the body? (Lee and Sasser-Coen 1996, p. 5).

This paper interrogates the politics of the Bondo at both the local and national levels, the activism around the Bondo by members of the society from two different camps—each of which claims cultural expertise on the society and the politics around the formulation of the National Strategy on the Reduction of FGM/C—and how these are interconnected. Central to this debate is the question of how cultural expertise is produced regarding Bondo society—what the Bondo means and how it is experienced in contemporary Sierra Leone. Like every culture, the Bondo's has changed over the years, moving from a one-year experience where matured girls are taught the art of traditional healing, home making, motherhood and sex education, to—in many cases—a one week experience where only excision takes place. The latter cases consequently trigger the highly political questions—if all that is left of Bondo culture is excision, how is it a culture worth maintaining? Why cannot the Bondo be revived with all its secret powers, but without the harmful practice of cutting? Moreover, in a globalized world where cultures are no longer clearly distinct—yet in which migrants decide to adhere to cultural practices that are criminalized in their host countries—the role of the cultural expert becomes increasingly important and vital for the administration of justice. It is therefore important that cultural expertise go beyond understanding the nuances of specific cultural practices, but also include an interrogation of the expert's political/ideological stance on the issue. In Sierra Leone where the issue of FGC is highly politicized, there seems to be no middle ground between pro- and anti-FGC campaigners and this certainly problematizes cultural expertise.

3. Methodology

Data for this paper was collected between 2016 and 2018 through interviews conducted with 10 members of the Forum Against Harmful Practice—a coalition of national and International organizations working towards ending female genital mutilation (FGM), reading reports, newspaper and academic articles and taking notes at various workshops and meetings held on the National Strategy on the Reduction of FGM/C. I tracked public discourses about FGC/M from both sides of the debate on TV, radio and other media sources. These included one-hour programs in which Soweis and members of the Sowei council were given the platform to explain their position—those with only anti-FGM/C campaigners, mixed panels and those with members of the public. These interviews were a common occurrence in the media and they opened up the conversation around FGM/C. FAHP members were interviewed to fully understand the nature and scope of their campaign, how they engaged with Bondo leaders and traditional authority and their role in the development of the Strategy.

4. The Politics of the Bondo

The use of the Bondo for political leverage and influence pre-dates independence and is as old as the society itself. Madam Yoko—paramount chief of the Kpa Mendes and the quintessential cultural expert on the Bondo—used the society to gain political power and influence during her reign in the 1800s. MacCormack (1974) posits that—as a Sowei and paramount chief—she used the society to consolidate her rule by pairing off beautiful Bondo initiates with powerful men. Existing within a hostile patriarchal environment, she bargained with patriarchy in many ways, to not only stay in power, but to become so powerful as to be considered almost an equal by other male rulers. What Kandiyoti (1988) refers to as "patriarchal bargaining" still forms the core of the Bondo women's access to power and influence. If they are not siding with paramount and local chiefs in the oppression of community members through fines and sanctions, they are selling the notions of solidarity and sodality among women of the society and thus presenting themselves as a formidable constituent to politicians vying for office. Since independence, politicians have used the strategy of financially supporting the mass initiation of young girls into the Bondo society, just before an election. They believe that this practice guarantees them large numbers of votes from community members whose financial burden is reduced through this act of "kindness." Initiating one's children into the Bondo society is often financially traumatic for many poor families who often end up in debt, as the Bondo can be a very expensive investment that arguably bears no fruitful gains. Initiators, chiefs and community leaders, as well as initiates, have to be lavished with food and gifts and cash payments have to be made to initiators and fees paid to paramount chiefs, who have to approve any ceremony in the community. Politicians willingly cover all of these costs, because they understand that in a society embedded in the traditional belief system of "akeh"—in which people believe that there are dire consequences for going back on one's word or betraying the trust of a person—or the belief of "one good turn deserves another," very few will dare to provoke what they consider to be the wrath of the gods by reneging on their promise to vote for these politicians. Interestingly, many of these politicians will pay to have other people's children excised, while they keep their own children out of the society and are still not held accountable by Soweis.

The fear of losing the rural vote has resulted in many politicians flirting with both sides of the argument. They may be against the FGM/C side of the Bondo, but publicly parrot the "respect for culture" mantra. This has in many ways hindered the promulgation of any progressive legislation on the practice and continues to pit women against each other. For example, the Child Rights bill of 2007 clearly specified a ban on FGM/C, but politicians were split on whether the FGM/C clause should be removed before it is enacted. In the end, the act was introduced, but without the FGM/C clause.

Since independence to date, not only has the political class—including women—failed to openly condemn the cutting aspect of the Bondo, but it has tacitly supported Bondo—not only by paying for mass initiation ceremonies, but by appointing/electing them to political positions such as community chairladies and party agents. Only in rare cases will a politician speak against the Bondo and that only happens when they know that they have an overwhelming influence over their constituents. At an anti-FGM/C event in 2015, the then minister of works—Kemoh Sesay—publicly condemned FGM/C and vowed to support the campaign for the abandonment of the practice. He also claimed that 70% of politicians are against the practice, do not excise their daughters and are "playing politics" with people's lives, because they believe that publicly condemning the practice is tantamount to political suicide.

Soweis have been able to capitalize on this undue fear of politicians to build a support base to counter anti-FGC discourse and advocacy[1]. They understand that the majority of proponents are uneducated and live in rural communities where these celebratory rites bring respite and joy to their lives of everyday drudgery. Soweis politicize the anti-FGM/C campaign, claiming first and foremost that—as practitioners—they have the sole rights to cultural expertise and further that those against cutting are stooges of the west, who no longer have any respect for "African ways" of being. As far as they are concerned, the questioning of the Bondo and its practices by lay persons and the encouragement of "non-natives/initiates" to discuss the practice is, in itself, abominable. The Bondo is not an issue discussed among initiates/members, let alone "airing" and sharing detailed information about the practice with "outsiders" and non-initiates. The evocations of race and location in this debate have provoked a number of political outbursts, which are typified by the recent impasse between anti-FGM campaigners and the most recent Minister of Gender Affairs on the validation of the draft Strategy on the Reduction of FGM/C. The minister—ironically a non-initiate—aligned herself with the Soweis, claiming that the anti-FGM campaign is a form of western propaganda which was not locally initiated, and which mainly exists because advocacy groups want to tap into funds being provided by western countries.

At the local level, the symbiotic relationships between the Bondo and the Poro and the Bondo and the chiefs are both political and economic. The paramount Chief is the only person who can authorize the construction of Bondo bushes or the initiation of girls. Bondo licenses, fees and fines for the infringement of the society's rules, form a huge chunk of revenue for Paramount chiefs. In addition, Soweis always have a coterie of young girls from whom chiefs can choose to become one of their many wives. As a part of traditional structures, Soweis often advise chiefs on issues affecting women in the community, broker peace and act as mediators between erring persons and the chief, thus building their social and political capital in the community.

Bondo leaders do play an important role in the exclusively male institution of the Poro, as the integral office of the "Mabole" is traditionally occupied by senior Bondo leaders, who are believed to have knowledge of the traditional healing herbs needed in the performance of Poro rituals. The reverence of the Bondo to the Poro society is articulated in a very popular saying in Sierra Leone—"Nar Bondo born Poro" (Bondo gave birth to Poro). However, this symbolic power is subordinated when a woman becomes a paramount chief and is expected to give up her Bondo membership to be initiated into the Poro, thereby clearly manifesting that leadership is masculine and male-dominated. Moreover, it has been argued that although collaboration between the Poro and the Bondo offers women some form of power, they are actually serving the interests of the patriarchal order by ensuring social cohesion through the formation of docile bodies (Phillips 1995; Pemunta and Tabenyang 2017; Fanthrope 2006). Through the practices of the Bondo, women's and girls' bodies and minds are trained and molded in the context of prevailing systems of power, presenting them with important lessons about feminine bodies, a woman's place, and desire. Women internalize these discourses and reproduce them, thereby maintaining oppressive, gendered social relations.

There was a great deal of hope that there would have been some major reforms to the Bondo society following the Ebola outbreak in 2015. This is because during the Ebola crisis, the paramount chiefs and some councils of Soweis—the custodians and experts of the culture—enacted by-laws that banned or postponed all forms of initiation ceremonies, with the dire consequences of fines and arrests if violated. This ban was reasonably effective because of the severity of the disease and the vigilance of the chiefs and Soweis. In addition, the president made a very hopeful statement during his speech on 7 November 2015 while declaring the end of Ebola, in which he stated that "a new beginning warrants

---

[1] I say undue fear because Rugiatu Neneh Turay—a very vocal anti FGM/C campaigner—12 years ago contested and won a council seat in Port Loko, where her organization the Amazonian Women's Initiative is located. Moreover, Sierra Leoneans—especially those in the rural areas—often vote in patterns whereby political party and ethnicity supersede every other consideration.

that traditional practices that have a negative impact on health, and which were discontinued during the outbreak, should not be returned to." Even though the president did not specifically name FGM/C, it was assumed by anti-FGM/C campaigners that FGM/C was one of such traditional practices to which he was referring. In as much as this statement was used as a campaign tool, there continues to be no political will to ban FGM/C—thus leaving the fight mainly between society sisters and non-cut advocates in the anti-FGM/C camp. In addition, two Sierra Leonean women scholars from an ethnic group that does not practice FGM/C—the Krios—have also contributed greatly to the understanding of the practice through research and advocacy.

5. When Society Women "Fight" Claiming Cultural Expertise and Human Rights

The debate around the merits and demerits of the Bondo (especially the FGC aspect of it) by pro- and anti-FGM/C activists in Sierra Leone is interestingly taking place mostly among members of the society. This is no surprise because, according to UNICEF (2016), 90% of Sierra Leonean women and girls have been excised and are thus members of the Bondo Society. Because women leading the campaign for the abandonment of the practice are members of the society, the insider/outsider labeling is difficult to make, hence the recourse to the branding of anti-FGM/C advocates as sell-outs to an imperialist agenda who limit the term "harmful traditional practice" to the excision of women whilst being mute on male circumcision. As far as they are concerned, the campaign against harmful traditional practices in Sierra Leone should not be limited to the Bondo society, but also extended to the Poro society.

Globally, the practice has generated heated debates between cultural relativists and Universalists. According to Renteln (2004), the doctrine of cultural relativism holds that there are no value judgments that are objectively falsifiable independent of specific cultures, and as such, moral judgments and social institutions in any one society are exempt from legitimate criticism by outsiders. On the other hand, the Universalist stance holds that certain individual rights are so fundamental to humankind that they should be upheld as universal rights whose breach is subject to condemnation and—in certain instances—punishment through legislative force (p. 127). Relativists thus see the practice of FGM/C from the vantage point of a ritual that signifies an important event in individual and group life. Whereas to many, like me, who subscribe to the Universalist position, the practice is viewed as an act of violence and violation of the human rights of women.

Although I identify with the Universalist view on the issue, I still question its sensationalization by international women's forums and agree with Toubia (1988)—a Sudanese scholar—who argues that these feminists have acted "as though they have suddenly discovered a dangerous epidemic, which they then sensationalized, in effect creating a backlash of over-sensitivity in the concerned communities. They have portrayed it as irrefutable evidence of barbarism and vulgarity of undeveloped countries. [and] it became a conclusive validation of the view of the primitiveness of Arabs, Muslims, and Africans all in one blow" (p. 101).

Cultural expertise are claimed by both sides of the divide, either because they have undergone the procedure, experienced the rituals or because they are the initiators and heads of the society. As cultural experts on the society, both sides of the campaign respect and believe in the importance and necessity of the Bondo society in the cultural identity of Sierra Leonean women. Where they differ is that anti-FGM/C activists want the society to abandon cutting, whereas the pro-FGM/C proponents believe that cutting is intrinsically intertwined with the Bondo and therefore find it difficult to imagine the Bondo without cutting. Both groups utilize human rights discourse, forgetting the fact that rights "including so-called universal ones, are not natural and eternal but always emergent and historically specific" and that rights always need to be contextualized, interpreted and negotiated (Cowan et al. 2001). Post-war reconstruction created a space for human rights to take hold in Sierra Leone and has offered an overarching, normative framework for civil society organizations to advocate for various rights. Thus, it is not surprising that there are claims of human rights violations from each side of the divide. The anti-FGM/C camp highlights the forceful initiation of children as a gross violation of the rights of children and evokes all the international and national treaties that protect the bodily integrity of women and children Sierra Leone has ratified, while the pro-FGM camp claims that the anti-FGM/C camp—who they have labelled the Zero Tolerance Propaganda Campaign—are violating their rights to cultural autonomy. Dr. Fuambai Sia Ahmadu—a Sierra Leonean born medical anthropologist and vocal Pro-FGM/C campaigner, who is the founder and intellectual guru of the Sierra Leone Women are Free to Choose (SLWAFC) movement, and who as recently as 6 February 2018 (International Day of Zero Tolerance on FGM) launched its first Female Circumcision Awareness Week in Sierra Leone in collaboration with the Sowei council—defends the pro-FGM/C campaign as such:

> I have been at the forefront of global debates and activism to counter the harmfulness and hypocrisy of FGM campaigns and to help restore the rights, autonomy and dignity of women who support or choose to uphold female circumcision as a religious or cultural practice. In Sierra Leone, this led to the formation of Sierra Leone Women are Free to Choose, to protect the fundamental constitutional and human rights of sowies as well as Bondo women who continue to uphold female circumcision as an important expression of gender identity or womanhood. (Interview 7 February 2018)

Anti-FGM/C campaign groups in Sierra Leone—such as the Forum against Harmful Practices (FAHP), which is a coalition of national and international non-governmental organizations working on the abandonment of FGM/C—have tried to incorporate a wide range of cultural custodians and experts including religious leaders, political leaders, medical professionals, paramount and section chiefs and the Soweis themselves in this campaign. They have placed FGM within a broader social justice agenda in which the government plays a central role in the protection of its citizens and have consistently used the Child Rights Act (2007)—which stipulates that the age of consent is 18 and criminalizes underage initiations—to hold the government and Soweis accountable for the initiation of underaged children. The campaign against the forceful initiation of children is very good, but falls short of addressing societal ostracism as the question remains—if a woman or girl's social identity is tied to the practice and she is ostracized for not participating, is that not also a form of force? The inability or unwillingness of the government—through the police and justice system—to enforce this aspect of the act shows how deeply engrained Sierra Leonenan society is in the belief systems of the Bondo society. It is common knowledge that ideologies and belief systems are most effective when most taken for granted. They resist correction and critique by making the status quo appear natural, "the way things are", rather than the result of human intervention and practice.

Anti-FGC campaigners also argue that the procedure is "a part of a continuum of patriarchal repression of female sexuality, which has been repressed in a variety of ways in all parts of the world throughout history and up to the present time" (Dorkenoo 1994, p. 29). They posit that when pro-campaigners argue that FGM is a culture-specific practice and a traditional practice that should be maintained, they fail to understand the might of the patriarchy and the status of FGM/C in this continuum of the patriarchal repression of female sexuality. They go on to point out the connections between the patriarchy and a string of repressive practices over time: the locking of the labials of female slaves with rings in ancient Rome; the chastity belts introduced by the Crusaders during the twelfth century; and, as late as the 1950s, the surgical removal of the clitoris as a "cure" for various ailments such as insomnia, sterility, lesbianism, masturbation and other supposed sexual deviances. They assert that the thousands of cosmetic surgeries performed today in Western societies indicate that the commodification, objectification and control of women are far from over. They cite the patriarchy as essential to the reasons why the bodies of women from different parts of the world, and from different religious, economic and educational backgrounds are "made" and expected to conform to societal expectations. In essence, they believe that sexualization in patriarchal societies involves a loss of female power, autonomy, and efficiency, and an imposition of norms and restrictions that are internalized by both men and women (Lee and Sasser-Coen 1996, p. 103).

Anti-FGM advocates tend to emphasize the health risks of the procedure, drawing their expertise from experience and research, both of which demonstrate that excised women and girls face many complications including urinary retention, bleeding, pain, septicemia and vaginal fistula, which in most instances lead to social ostracism and divorce. They argue that the procedure is mainly performed on children as young as one—who actually have limited voices or power—who are forced to undergo a procedure that can potentially leave them physically and emotionally traumatized. They see women's bodies as sites of struggle that involve both compliance and resistance to normalizing discourses and understand that the control of women's bodies in both public and private spaces is essential for the maintenance of patriarchal societies.

As convincing as the arguments raised by anti-FGC campaigners are, those who vehemently fight against its abolition are women and not men. It will therefore be simplistic to present a picture of the African woman as wholly subservient, passive, and "voiceless"; one whose sexual and reproductive potential is controlled by men and whose genitals are mutilated in silence without protest. Thus, because women have the upper hand in determining when, how, and where a girl will be excised, it is often difficult to make people understand that the practice is based on a patriarchal value system. In Sierra Leone, Bondo women yield power not only because they alone perform these procedures, but also because they have been able to bargain with the patriarchy in varied ways. Abusharaf (2000) posits that in the Sudan, the ritual becomes an important affirmation of one generation of women's authority over another. She cautions that this should not be dismissed as an expression of false consciousness, in which women perpetrate their own subjugation, nor can the motive behind FGM/C be traced to a single patriarchal value.

Pro-FGM/C campaigners see the procedure as an important marker in the transition to adult femininity, purity, and marriageability and—even though this is far from the reality—see the Bondo bush as a place where initiates are taught the art of home keeping, good social relations with in-laws, sex education, child-bearing and aspects of motherhood and traditional medicine. The organizing of initiators into a structured body called the Sowei council—formed in 1993 and headquartered in Freetown, but with branches in all the districts—gave this group a formal public presence that can insert itself to counter on-going anti-FGC rhetoric and actions. Since its formation, Soweis have been formally invited to conferences and workshops, and have been able to engage the media to advocate on their own behalf. The more visibility they gained, the more defiant they have become, and the more the political wind blew in their favor, the more emboldened they have become. What seems to aggravate the Soweis the most is that the "secret" of the Bondo is now in the public sphere (media, meetings, workshops, etc.) and is discussed by non-initiates and non-experts. This they see as an abuse of their culture and a violation of their right to cultural integrity.

Irrespective of the WHO's definition that—by medical standards—the removal of a healthy normal organ from a human body when there is no medical or aesthetic reason is a mutilation, pro-FGC campaigners of Bondo in Sierra Leone take offence to the word mutilation and consider it a racist and degrading epithet for an experience they find somehow empowering. They argue that the term "mutilation" does not necessarily differentiate between the forms and degree of severity practiced by different societies. As Ahmadu (2018) argues:

> The fact is that the majority of circumcised women support female circumcision just like the majority of circumcised men support male circumcision. For most of the population of women in Sierra Leone, the term FGM is a huge affront to our identity and an unacceptable insult against us, our mothers and female elders. (Interview 7 February 2018)

The pro-campaigners further argue that the use of "choice" by western anti-FGM campaigners is very selective, especially in relation to cosmetic surgery and FGC. They point out that there is an overwhelming silence on acts of "mutilation" going on in the western world through cosmetic surgeries such as labia reduction and other forms of "designer vagina" surgeries. Many of these surgeries, like FGC, they argue, are performed on underaged girls for whom parental consent is deemed enough before surgeries take place. Thus, the question they ask is—why is parental consent by parents of young girls who undergo FGC not enough? Dr. Fuambai Sia Ahmadu (2016) in another interview had this to say on the issue:

> While our African governments are busy succumbing to pressure from western women to outlaw our traditional female genital aesthetic practices, western countries have developed a flourishing female genital cosmetic surgery industry, using our own operations as the aesthetic standard.
>
> And, instead of fighting to defend the rights of our mothers and grandmothers, many of us who are western educated have given carte blanche for them to be stripped, degraded and punished by and for the sake of the very white women whose own mothers and daughters are now freely opting for the same procedures.
>
> I have always said, Sierra Leone is the ground zero where modern western feminism meets the power of ancient Bondo society. As you can see, I've placed my bets on Bondo. (Interview 8 February 2016)

The racial undertones and bias of the anti-FGM/C campaign have also been highlighted by many scholars. For example, Ehrenreich and Barr (2005) argue that

> "... the mainstream anti-FGC position is premised upon an orientalizing construction of FGC societies as primitive, patriarchal, and barbaric, and of female circumcision as a harmful, unnecessary cultural practice based on patriarchal gender norms and ritualistic beliefs. ... Lambasting African societies and practices (while failing to critique similar practices in the United States) ... essentially implies that North American understandings of the body are "scientific" (i.e., rational, civilized, and based on universally acknowledged expertise), while African understandings are "cultural" (i.e., superstitious, un-civilized, and based on false, socially constructed beliefs). [Yet] neither of these depictions is accurate. North American medicine is not free of cultural influence, and FGC practices are not bound by culture—at least not in the uniform way imagined by opponents". (Cited in Earp 2014)

6. The National Strategy for the Reduction of FGM/C: A Site of Contestation

In order to fulfill its obligations as a signatory to the Convention on the Elimination of Discrimination against Women (CEDAW), the Convention of the Rights of the Child (CRC) and the Maputo Protocol, the government—with the support of UNICEF, through its Minister of Social Welfare Gender and Children's Affairs (MSWGCA)—in 2014 commissioned the development of a National Strategy for the Reduction of FGM/C (2016–2020), with three key pillars: Pillar 1—Creating an Enabling Environment for FGM/C abandonment; Pillar 2—Strengthening National Capacities to prevent FGM/C and care for those living with FGM/C; and pillar 3—Sustained Community Commitment to FGM/C abandonment. The position of the government is made clear in the introduction to the strategy which states that "The Government of Sierra Leone, whilst upholding the noble values of the Institution of Bondo recognizes the practice of FGM/C, which is presently part of the initiation activities for Bondo membership, as a health burden and a violation of the human rights of children and women" (National Strategy 2016). Recognizing the challenge, the government further states in the foreword that,

> We are aware that postponing FGM/C does not mean reduction. For us to achieve reduction, we need to reduce the incidence of new cases of girls undergoing FGM/C. In this strategy, we consider measures which whilst celebrating and upholding the wholesome aspects of the Bondo Institution seek to remove the harm from the initiation ceremony and create alternative new spaces where adolescent girls can be publicly recognised as women and are identified with their ethnic groups. (National Strategy 2016)

Even as sensitive to the wishes of both sides of the divide as the document has tried to be, it has become the most contentious document in the FGM/C debate and is still on the shelves in the Ministry, yet to be validated and implemented. The politics around the strategy continues to deepen the divide between both camps, with each hoping for a Minister that is sympathetic to its cause.

While the anti-FGM/C camp claims that the process was very inclusive, the pro- camp insist that it was not and that the views of practitioners were not taken into consideration. Reports, however, show that in January 2014, validation workshops were conducted in all 13 administrative districts in the country to ensure the buy-in of all stakeholders—men, women, Soweis, MPs, paramount and other chiefs, religious and political leaders. The aim was for each group to play its own role towards the abandonment of the practice. However, taking into consideration the number of Soweis and Bondo bushes, the argument that many would not have been reached via a single district validation exercise remains valid. For such a contentious issue, continuous engagement is imperative.

The government's recognition of the practice as a violation of international human rights laws and its call for the abandonment of cutting in the rituals of the society are big bones of contention that do not sit well with pro- campaigners. This places responsibility for the practice squarely with the state, which has the duty to ensure that its citizens enjoy full human rights and that means enforcing the law by persecuting violators.

7. Conclusions

In the Sierra Leonean context, the "special knowledge" of "so-called 'cultural brokers'" is highly mediated by a subjective position that is politically and ideologically driven. It is almost impossible for such brokers not to take sides if and when called upon to provide expert testimony. The fact remains that the differing views between pro- and anti-FGC campaigners in Sierra Leone fail to recognize that "cultural expertise rests on the ability to distinguish and valorise different cultural forms in a way that resonates with others possessing the same expertise, meaning expert judgements are as much of other people's judgements as of the forms in question." (Kontoyannis and Christos 2010, p. 747). Both camps are so convinced about their positions that, as things stand, no middle ground seems to be feasible, excepting the existence of a strong political will to drive the process. A starting point is a genuine acceptance of the age of consent and the enforcement of the law without political interference. It is apparent that on the level of practice, there remains a diminishing degree of choice for communities and individuals whose traditions have become irrevocably situated in the public arena and—on the level of discourse—silence on the topic no longer seems to be an option, and the choice that remains is between informed and non-informed discussions (Shell-Duncan and Hernlund 2000, p. 3). In Sierra Leone, the debate has permeated every corner and level of society, making it imperative for a critical interrogation of the cultural expertise of both groups and the political and economic dynamics that keep the "fight" going. Why would a group (pro-FGC) so violently defend a society that has over the years abandoned rituals and practices that were believed to make them powerful, but continue to hold on tightly to just one ritual (cutting) that has been described as harmful? And why would another group (anti-FGC) risk their lives, as well as social and political capital to condemn a practice that has been in existence for hundreds of years and which is said to be supported by the majority of Sierra Leoneans? The fact of the matter is that traditional practices are all liable to change—slavery, corsets, and foot binding were once thought to be essential elements of cultures in some parts of the world. Change is already happening in relation to the Bondo, as it is already being threatened by the global anti-female circumcision discourse which is not going to change any time soon. Choice and the age of consent have become central to the debate and that was not the case a few decades ago. The arguments of both sides of the divide are couched in the human rights discourse of choice. The question therefore is how do we situate cultural expertise within the human rights discourse in cases where human rights is evoked to defend traditional practices that have been deemed harmful in non-practicing societies?

Funding: EURO-EXPERT-ERC funded project 681814 sponsored the presentation of this essay at the conference entitled "Cultural Expertise in Ancient and Modern History" convened in Oxford by the principal investigator, Livia Holden.

Conflicts of Interest: The author declares no conflict of interest.

References

Abusharaf, Rogaia Mustafa. 2000. Revisionist feminist discourses on infibulation: Responses from Sudanese Feminists. In *Female "Circumcision" in Africa: Culture, Controversy, and Change*. Edited by Bettina Shell-Duncan and Ylva Herlun. Boulder: Lynne Reinner Publishers.

Ahmadu, Sia. 2016. Female circumcision—Women must have the right to choose. *The Sierra Leone Telegraph*. Available online: http://www.thesierraleonetelegraph.com/female-circumcision-women-must-have-the-right-to-choose-says-dr-fuambai-sia-ahmadu/ (accessed on 9 June 2018).

Ahmadu, Sia. 2018. Female Circumcision Awareness Week. *The Sierra Leone Telegraph*. February 7. Available online: http://www.thesierraleonetelegraph.com/female-circumcision-awareness-week-dr-fuambai-sia-ahmadu-speaks/ (accessed on 9 June 2018).

Bjalkander, Awolabi, Donald S. Grant, Vanja Berggren, Heli Bathija, and Lars Almroth. 2013. Female Genital Mutilation in Sierra Leone: Forms, Reliability of Reported Status, and Accuracy of Related Demographic and Health Survey Questions. *Obstetrics and Gynecology International* 2013: 680926. [CrossRef] [PubMed]

Bosire, Obara Tom. 2012. The Bondo Secret Society: Female Circumcision and the Sierra Leonean State. Ph.D. thesis, University of Glasgow, Glasgow, UK.

Cowan, Jane K., Marie-Benedicte Dembour, and Richard A. Wilson, eds. 2001. *Culture and Rights: Anthropological Perspectives*. Cambridge: Cambridge University Press.

Dorkenoo, Efua. 1994. *Cutting the Rose. Female Genital Mutilation: The Practice and Its Prevention*. London: Minority Rights Publications.

Earp, Brian D. 2014. Female Genital Mutilation (FGM) and Male Circumcision: Should There Be a Separate Ethical Discourse? Practical Ethics. University of Oxford. Available online: https://www.academia.edu/8817976/Female_genital_mutilation_FGM_and_male_circumcision_Should_there_be_a_separate_ethical_discourse (accessed on 15 June 2018). [CrossRef]

Ehrenreich, Nancy, and Mark Barr. 2005. Intersex surgery, female genital cutting, and the selective condemnation of cultural practices. *Harvard Civil Rights-Civil Liberties Law Review* 40: 71–539.

Fanthrope, Richard. 2006. On the limits of liberal peace: Chiefs and democratic decentralization in post-war Sierra Leone. *African Affairs* 105: 27–49. [CrossRef]

Kandiyoti, Deniz. 1988. Bargaining with patriarchy. *Gender and Society* 6: 274–90. [CrossRef]

Kontoyannis, Maria, and Katsetos Christos. 2010. Female genital mutilation. *Health Science Journals* 41: 31–36.

Lee, Janet, and Jennifer Sasser-Coen. 1996. *Blood Stories: Menarche and the politics of the Female Body in Contemporary U.S. Society*. New York and London: Routledge.

MacCormack, Carol. 1974. *Madam Yoko: Ruler of the Kpa Mende Confederacy*. Edited by Carol MacCormack. Stanford: Stanford University Press.

Mgbako, Chi, Meghna Saxena, Cave Anna, and Nasim Farjad. 2010. Penetrating the Silence in Sierra Leone: A Blueprint for the Eradication of Female Genital Mutilation. *Harvard Human Rights Journal* 23: 111–40.

Sierra Leone National Strategy for the Reduction of FGM/C (2016–2020)- Draft 3. 2016. Freetown: Government of Sierra Leone.

Pemunta, Ngambouk Vitalis, and Tabi Chama-James Tabenyang. 2017. Cultural Power, ritual symbolism and human rights violation in Sierra Leone. *Cogent Social Sciences* 3: 1295549. [CrossRef]

Phillips, Ruth B. 1995. *Representing Woman: Sande Masquerades of the Mende of Sierra Leone*. Berkeley: University of California.

Renteln, Alison Dundes. 2004. *The Culture of Defense*. Oxford: Oxford University Press.

Shell-Duncan, Bettina, and Ylva Hernlund. 2000. *Female "Circumcision" in Africa: Culture, Controversy, and Change*. Boulder: Lynne Reinner Publishers.

Sulkin, Londono. 2009. Disputing the Myth of the Sexual Dysfunction of Circumcised Women: An Interview with Fuambai S. Ahmadu by Richard A. *Shweder Anthropology Today* 25: 14–17.

Toubia, N. 1988. Women and Health. In *Sudan in Women of the Arab World: The Coming Challenge*. Edited by Nahid Toubia. London: Zed Books, p. 101.

UNICEF. 2016. Sierra Leone Statistical Profile on Female Genital Mutilation/Cutting. Data and Analytics Section—Division of Data, Research and Policy UNICEF, 3 UN Plaza, New York, 10017. Available online: https://data.unicef.org/wpcontent/uploads/country_profiles/Sierra%20Leone/FGMC_SLE.pdf (accessed on 4 March 2018).

© 2019 by the author. Licensee MDPI, Basel, Switzerland. This article is an open access article distributed under the terms and conditions of the Creative Commons Attribution (CC BY) license (http://creativecommons.org/licenses/by/4.0/).

MDPI
St. Alban-Anlage 66
4052 Basel
Switzerland
Tel. +41 61 683 77 34
Fax +41 61 302 89 18
www.mdpi.com

Laws Editorial Office
E-mail: laws@mdpi.com
www.mdpi.com/journal/laws

www.ingramcontent.com/pod-product-compliance
Lightning Source LLC
Chambersburg PA
CBHW040225040426
42333CB00052B/3372